REBORN FOR LOVE

A CASE SUGGESTIVE
OF REINCARNATION

HERNANI GUIMARÃES ANDRADE

 **Roundtable** Publishing
London 2010

 **Roundtable** Publishing
roundtable.uk@gmail.com
London 2010

Acknowledgements
The publisher wishes to thank the
Society for Psychical Research and the Tate Bequest
for their financial assistance.

All profits received from this publication will be employed by Roundtable Publishing
Ltd for the publishing of further books.

The Publisher's policy is to use paper manufactured from sustainable forests.

CONTENTS

Chapter III - Hypothesis That Explains Kilden Alexandre's Memories And Behaviour

Chapter IV

Acknowledgments

The author is deeply grateful to the following people, whose valued help contributed decisively to the realisation of this book:

Luiz Antônio Brasil for his collaboration and help in obtaining the subject family's data, in São João del Rey;

Suzuko Hashizume and Maria das Graças de Souza for their help in preparing and revising the original edition of this book;

Elsie Dubugras and Luiz Carlos Bojikian for their translation of this book from Portuguese to English;

Special thanks to 'Marine Waterloo' and to her previous personality, whose names and current address are necessarily withheld for ethical reasons;

Finally, our immense gratitude to Dr. Marlene Rossi Severino Nobre for her magnificent preface, which enhances this modest work.

Bauru, Spring, 2002.
Hernani Guimarães Andrade

To an unforgettable master and friend
JOSÉ DE FREITAS NOBRE,
whose ethical and civic virtues represent
a paradigm to be followed by all of us.

BY THE SAME AUTHOR

A Teoria Corpuscular do Espírito. Author, 1958.

Novos Rumos à Experimentação Espírita. Author, 1960.

Parapsicologia Experimental. Editora Pensamento, São Paulo, 1967.

O Caso Ruytemberg Rocha. IBPP Monograph No 1, 1971.

The Ruytemberg Rocha Case. IBPP Monograph No l, 1973 (in English)

A Case Suggestive of Reincarnation: Jacira & Ronaldo. IBPP Monograph No 3, 1980. (in English)

A Matéria Psi. Casa Editora O Clarim, Matão, 1972 .

Morte, Renascimento Evolução: Uma Biologia Transcendental. Editora Pensamento, São Paulo, 1983.

Muerte, Renacimiento, Evolucion: Una Biología Trascendental. Ediciones CIMA, Caracas,1993. (in Spanish).

Espírito, Perispírito e Alma: Ensaio Sobre o Modelo Organizador Biológico. Editora Pensamento, São Paulo, 1984.

Psi Quântico. Uma Extensão dos Conceitos Quânticos e Atômicos à Idéia do Espírito. Editora Pensamento, São Paulo, 1986.

Reencarnação no Brasil (Oito Casos que Sugerem Renascimento). Casa Editora O Clarim, Matão, 1988.

Ocho Casos de Reencarnacion. Editora Rivail, Santafé de Bogotá, 1994 (in Spanish).

Poltergeist (Algumas de Suas Ocorrências no Brasil). Editora Pensamento, São Paulo, 1989

Transcomunicação Instrumental – TCI. (pseudonym Karl W. Goldstein) Editora Jornalística FE, 1992.

Você, o Poltergeist e os Locais Mal Assombrados. Editora Didier, Votuporanga, 1995.

A Transcomunicação Atraves dos Tempos. Editora FE, São Paulo, 1997.

Morte – Uma Luz no Fim do Túnel. Editora FE, São Paulo, 1999.

Parapsicologia – Uma Visão Panorâmica. Editora FE, São Paulo, 2002.

Você e a Reencarnação. CEAC Editora, Bauru, 2002.

A Mente Move a Matéria. Editora FE, São Paulo, 2005.

PREFACE

Readers familiar with Hernani Guimarães Andrade's work will probably find the title of this monograph strange. After all, the author is the president of the Brazilian Institute For Psychobiophysical Research (IBPP – Instituto Brasileiro de Pesquisas Psicobiofísicas) and has always taken an ethical, rigorous and impartial approach, his research into poltergeists and reincarnation being considered classics of parapsychological investigation.

However, the author is aware of this possible strangeness and emphasises in the epilogue that "the present case, besides having a purely scientific aspect, has a component of sentimental, dramatic and deeply human nature. Within it there are two people connected by strong mutual affection. Once reincarnation is demonstrated, at least in the case we are studying, it seems to show clearly that the feelings which intervene in human relationships are perpetual."

Further on he admits "We have enough experience of the scientific 'establishment' to calculate the risk we run of invalidating the present work, or reducing its value and credibility, just by focusing on this aspect. However, in this case we believe it is justifiable to do so."

Thus, Hernani deliberately opts for risk, stressing - based on scientific data - the dominant power of feelings in the conduct of human existence. In this aspect, he fulfills the same mission as the eminent physicist and humanist Fritjof Capra, author of the excellent works The Tao of Physics and Turning Point, since he seeks the complementarity of the two archetype poles of Taoism : Yin and Yang, love and wisdom, that is essential for the equilibrium of the human being.

The author's opinion is that the rigour of meticulous, objective research should not exclude emphasis on feelings, mainly because they intervene in human relationships in a perennial manner. With this deliberate approach, this book contributes to a change in the mechanical-reductionist paradigm of science that still remains unchanged in most academic circles.

The important contribution that reincarnation research makes to psychoanalysis should be strongly emphasised. Without the recognition that man is born, lives again and always improves, obeying a natural biological law, the theories of Freud and his successors will never make progress or increase their ability to help the human mind.

A brief psychoanalytic reading of the present case, mainly based on a story presented in a charming and touching way by Mrs. Marine Waterloo, makes one think of a badly resolved Oedipus complex leading to Kilden's difficulty in learning to read.

Why does Kilden Alexandre and not Kildary have differences and disagreements with their father? Psychoanalysts will say that their libidos are different, and that their expression through unconscious channels depends on the personality of each one, on the quantum of death or life instinct each one carries since conception, and on the way they have lived their different phases - oral, anal and phallic, especially in their first six years. With reincarnation, the explanation is much more complete, and all pieces of the puzzle fit. Actually, each son has a unique history, and affective and emotional connections with his parents, which remain attached to the thread of successive incarnations.

It is also clear that Marcinho, D. Marine's husband, has difficulty in accepting Father Jonathan, and the converse was true to some extent. The feeling of dislike comes up again, involving Marcinho and Kilden. Everything indicates that one of the purposes of this incarnation, for both of them, is the search for reciprocal forgiveness.

Psychoanalysis can undoubtedly help a lot, but complete success will only be reached with the transformation of this dislike into love, and the foundations of this change are in to be found in Jesus' teaching, above all in our daily striving towards renewal.

That is why the techniques for affective/egoist disentanglement are so successful, as described in the extensive literature of Spiritism. Yet there is another important aspect of this research: the presence of phobias linked to events in other existences.

Hernani has already referred to this discovery in another notable work of his, Reencarnação no Brasil, (Reincarnation in Brazil), especially in the case of Jacira and Ronaldo. Young Ronaldo, 28 years old, committed suicide by drinking poison dissolved in guaraná (a Brazilian soft drink). When he reincarnated as Jacira, he felt strong aversion for liquids of red or similar colour. In this book, he reminds us that phobias can be related to objects, colours, foods, scenes, animals and words, including names, as observed in one of the episodes of Jonathan and Kilden's case.

The files of the National Institute for Past-Life Therapy (INTVP), headed by Dr. Maria Júlia de Morais Prieto Peres, whose psychotherapic technique is based on reincarnation, also contain cases in which phobias are linked to traumatic events in previous lives.

Dr. Ian Stevenson was able to to verify the same incidence of phobias in children that remembered previous lives (Children Who Remember Previous Lives, The University Press of Virginia, USA, 1987, p.220). He recorded more than 2000 cases, in 23 of which people killed themselves in their previous lives, four of them accidentally, two by committing suicide to avoid being captured by the police, and the remaining 17 for personal reasons. Besides verifying that those people had not been in hell for centuries, Dr. Stevenson observed that many of this group had phobias related to the instrument of the suicide, such as weapons or poison.

In the same book he dedicates a chapter (nine) to the study of infancy and early childhood phobias, and notes the difficulties that child psychiatrists and parents have in explaining some of those cases that are not derived from any known trauma, and do not seem to be imitations of a similar existent fear in another member of the family.

Dr. Stevenson reminds us that some psychiatrists attribute inexplicable phobias to a symbolic displacement of the fear that a person has of another to an animal or object. They follow the same line as Freud, who interpreted little Hans' phobia for horses as terror of his own father. But the psychiatrist and researcher of reincarnation is convinced, based on the evidence, that many phobias cannot be explained if we confine their cause to the present life.

As we can see, meticulous researchers of reincarnation such as Ian Stevenson and Hernani Guimarães Andrade have made an enormous contribution to the change in the materialistic paradigm on which science is based. After all, the human organism is a living system guided by a Spirit, whose components are all interlinked and interdependent, being a integrated portion of larger systems, continuously interacting with the physical and social environment as well as the spiritual world, also being constantly affected by them, and for its time, being able to modify and act on them.

Maybe Carl Gustav Jung was the first to understand the classic psychology behind those wider concepts. In "Aion" he foresaw that nuclear physics and the psychology of the unconscious would get closer and closer together. He affirmed that psyche and matter exist in the same world, sharing the same experiences; thus he concludes that the final agreement between physical and psychological concepts would come as the natural consequence of scientific development.

According to him Mind "arises from an unconscious psyche that is older than it is and continues to function together with it or even in spite of it". Jung distinguished two spheres in the unconscious psyche: a personal unconscious, belonging to the individual and a collective unconscious, a deeper stratum of the psyche common to all humanity. According to him, genuine spirituality is an integral part of the human psyche and is shown in different degrees in each individual.

Cases that suggest reincarnation confirm that the psyche stays alive in spite of bodily death. In this monograph that is so evident that my poor foreword is perfectly dispensable. Only a kind author could think that it would be of some value.

Hernani Guimarães Andrade already had the opportunity to affirm (Folha Espírita, October, 1991) that "the materialistic conception concerning our underlying reality is destroying man and planet Earth. We have to change and the only way is the search for Spiritualism and its correlated themes".

Here we have a book that deals with the Spirit, and still more, celebrates love between souls. Inspired by this sublime feeling, the heavens and Earth are populated by creatures looking for each other as bees seek nectar in the desire to find its inexhaustible source - God.

São Paulo, 1994.
Marlene Nobre

INTRODUCTION

"Thinking better, if we adopt the most extreme and mystic Gnostic thesis of Spirit-that-turns-into-matter-and-later-dominates-it, we will be less far from the truth than if we adhere to the extremist scientific thesis of Matter-that-manufactures-the-Spirit ".

Raymond Ruyer (1974)

(La Gnose de Princeton)

A PRECIOUS LETTER

We usually receive numerous and varied pieces of mail - letters from all over the world as well as from our country. Every day we carry out the ritual, which we consider to be sacred, of opening and reading them, and drafting the answers. They generally are of the type we might call "begging-letters", as most of them are asking for something, such as information, books, monographs or copies of articles or photographs, or they might ask for opinions of works sent to us by their author sometimes with a request for a foreword. Although this has become both habitual and gratifying, it does take up much of the available reserve of time we can count on from now on, due to our advanced age.

Even so, it is a worthy task, since some letters are not begging but donating. One such letter was delivered on November 6th, 1990, and this is what it had to say:

"I am an active Spiritist here in the state of Minas Gerais, where studying and practising the doctrines of Kardec tends to lead to a degree of isolation."

He complained about the difficulties caused by the lack of culture that our country suffers, even in the spiritist environment. However, he seemed resigned to the fact that the situation was not going to change for some time.

"Even so, I'm not complaining, and understand that each of us is where we should be."

He went on to tell us how he had heard of us and our interest in research into paranormal facts, after reading some of our writings. He ended his letter:

"Another reason why I am writing is that I am studying a case which seems to suggest reincarnation. Knowing about your interest in this and the research into it that you have done together with Dr. Ian Stevenson, I am asking if you would like to know more about this case. If so, please let me know what information you need and how you would like to proceed. It's about a boy of ten who is identifying himself with an adult who died in 1972.

"Yours, etc
Luiz Antonio Brasil

This valuable letter was posted in São João del Rei, Minas Gerais on November 1st, 1990 and delivered on the 6th. It was not the first letter we had received telling us about some paranormal event, especially about a case suggestive of reincarnation. Generally the communicants of such cases show great enthusiasm and conviction, requesting urgent instructions on how to proceed in order to research them appropriately. Some even want to know how to publish their results immediately. Others promise to send reports and 'proofs' of their case as soon as they receive instructions.

Yet what happens is that the investigation of paranormal phenomena such as reincarnation calls for some ability on the part of the researcher, and a lot of patience and previous knowledge of the subject, acquired from reading and deeper studies. So nearly always we send off our extensive instruction material and hear no more. The enthusiasm of would-be investigators tends to cool when they realise just what is involved in strictly scientific research, and find that one cannot investigate a complex case overnight, but needs to take time in order to obtain the evidence needed to establish the truth of the matter in question.

Bearing this in mind, we immediately sent off the material our correspondent asked for, without much hope of getting a worthwhile reply. On November 11th we sent him a package containing detailed instructions for research of reincarnation-type cases, questionnaire forms, and a copy of our report on the Jacyra/Ronaldo case as an example of a case that had already been studied and solved.

We also sent a letter in which we guaranteed that our Institute would maintain strict confidentiality regarding the identity of those involved, and we added that we would be glad to answer any further questions.

THE SURPRISE

On December 4th, 1990, just 23 days after we had sent our answer to Luiz Antônio Brasil's letter, we received the preliminary research material we had asked for. When we saw his full and meticulous report, we couldn't believe what we were seeing. There in front of us were full details of the case since its inception, all questionnaires appropriately answered, plus a concise account of the case, all neatly typed. It was too good to be true.

So, thanks to our colleague's exceptional efficiency, we were able to start work at once on this case, which we would not have been able to do without his help.

São João del Rei is about 800km (500 miles) from Bauru. It took us twelve hours to get there by car. There now follows a full account of what we were able to record during our prolonged investigation of this case.

CHAPTER I

HISTORICAL

"Since 1961, one of us (I.S.) has researched in India and other places cases of people (usually children) who affirm that they have lived before and remember details of such previous lives..." Prof. Ian Stevenson, MD. (Research in Parapsychology, 1979, p. 72)

On the morning of July 24th, 1992, we paid our first visit to D. Marine and her family. It was a great success.

She and her husband Marcinho have six children - two sons and four daughters. They are all good looking and very well behaved. The eldest son, then 20 years old, is a seminarist. Kilden is the fourth son and was 11 years old. He is a bright, attractive and communicative kid. We talked with him for a long time but noticed that his memories of previous lives had disappeared, perhaps hidden in his subconscious mind.

D. Marine Waterloo is a very intelligent and well educated woman. She graduated in Pedagogy, has published several books and has a good position in the cultural society of São João del Rey. She greeted us warmly and offered to help us as much as possible. Thanks to her invaluable help it was possible to write this book.

D. Marine is a born writer and she immediately offered to give us a detailed written report on her son's case. We then agreed that she would answer our questions, maintain correspondence in order to fill up the gaps in the report and the questionnaire. She did exactly what she had promised to do, and more. We are indeed grateful to this extraordinary lady.

I will start with the whole of Marine Waterloo's report on the background and details of the case of Kilden and Jonathan. But first I should make it clear that the Brazilian Institute for Psychobiophysical Research (IBPP) obeys strictly ethical principles, not revealing the identity of its subjects and their respective families. For this reason, the real names and locations of those involved are deliberately changed or disguised by the use of false names and monograms. Any resemblance that might lead to the identification of a place or a well-known person would be due to mere chance or mistaken interpretation.

Another detail has to do with the previous personality. As this was a respected priest of the Roman Catholic Church, it might seem to those who are sensitive in regard to religious discrimination that this report intends to demoralise the clergy of that church. It must be made clear right away that this is absolutely not its purpose. Although I do not subscribe to any religion, I respect all of them. If I wished to attack any religious creed, I would do so openly on a basis of logic and rational discussion and not in any underhand or malicious way.

Here, then, is Dona Marine Waterloo's account of the background to the case of Kilden/Jonathan.

INTRODUCTION

PART ONE

After the sounding of the second bell I left the bedroom and walked down the steps on the way to the chapel. It was the start of the school year of 1968. All the boarders, including some new ones, were already in the High School.

On entering the chapel I was surprised to see that our last year's chaplain was not there. In his place was a darker skinned priest with curly hair who awaited us, smiling.

There was a general surprise. Some seemed disappointed and some of the younger ones started to laugh. He also laughed and greeted some, who were from his home town, by name. Yet there was a feeling of general dissatisfaction during Mass. Nobody except the Sisters prayed or sang properly.

After Mass, we all went to the dining room and had our coffee before our first classes of the year. The talk was all about the change of chaplain. Many did not agree because they adored the former one, while others who came from the new one's home town could not stand him, though I only learned this later. Some of them thought he was so ugly that they hated him at first sight, which I found ridiculously childish. Why judge people by their looks? What difference would it make to the Sacred Rite, if the priest was physically ugly? And what impressed me even more was that the senior girls, some of them members of distinguished families and even relatives of nuns, should behave in such a mean way.

We were still in the dining room in that uncharitable climate when the new chaplain came in. (The former one never visited our dining room). My colleagues' indignation increased and they all started chattering and muttering in whispers.

'Good morning. Good morning. How are you, D. Maria?'

'Good morning.' Only some four of us answered.

'So many girls! How many are you?'

'Ninety-six', said the assistant nun, who had noticed the girls' hostility.

She had a few words with the chaplain, and then he said 'Good-bye. Work hard', smiled and left the room.

Everyone remained silent. It was a heavy, uneasy and unpleasant silence. Then one of my more audacious friends got up and said:

'What did the poor priest do to be treated in this manner'.

She was greeted by a chorus of jeers and catcalls.

'Oh, grow up!' my friend yelled. 'Where's your sense of decency?'

Just then the bell for classes rang, and we left the dining room in silence and went to our respective classrooms.

I was starting my second year of high school. My enthusiasm, wish to learn, joy of living and, the desire to succeed made me a responsible and self-confident girl.

Our first class was Portuguese, with the same teacher we had the year before. Sister Antônia entered smiling and blushing as always, and greeted us.

'Does anyone remember what I said to you several times last year?', she began. When Sister Antônia spoke to us, even when she was angry, she always smiled and her deep and dark green eyes would penetrate the soul.

I raised my hand.

'Yes, Marine?'

I stood up and said in a solemn voice:

'The greatest losers are those who have never lost, because they are afraid to lose.' It was my favourite proverb.

'Very good. Don't forget it, girls!'

During the class, my friend Edilene intrigued me by saying she had something to tell me, but only when the time was right.

The days went by and the girls' dissatisfaction increased. It was during this time that I discovered how empty people could be and how deep-rooted racism is in Brazil. They would talk about Father Jonathan all day long - that was his name, Jonathan.

It didn't bother me that they liked one chaplain more than the other. I had never spoken to the old one, Father Jodi. He was a serious and pious man, always very nice and well liked, though he never played games with us or tried to get to know us.

Father Jonathan was just the opposite. Right from the first day he mixed with the girls and played with all of them, pretending that he did not see their ironic smiles or feel their unfounded dislike.

During Mass, which was celebrated every day at 6:30 am,

whispers and looks could be noticed amongst the girls. It was a strange and disagreeable climate. Due to this disrespectful behaviour the Masses celebrated by Father Jonathan were like circus performances. We thought the nuns would take steps to change the chaplain. But nothing happened.

Within a month or so, however, Father Jonathan had already won almost all of us over. At that time I thought it was brave of him to plunge into such a totally hostile environment. Now, however, I know that it was not a case of bravery. Behind that dark man who was despised by all, there was a virtue too little appreciated in our time: humility. That rather unattractive body, with its curly hair and unerudite way of talking, housed a pure and simple soul.

Before we got to know our new chaplain, we only knew those stern priests who shut themselves in the Sacristy and went away after Mass. They had never tried to get to know us, ask our names, where we were born, and so on. Father Jonathan caused quite a stir in our 'whited sepulchre'.

One day during our lunch break, Sister Nivalda came up to me and said:

'I have noticed something that saddens me, Marine.'

'What is it, Sister Nivalda?' I asked her, rather alarmed because I was just leaning against a pillar in the corridor, pretending I was watching a game of volleyball.

'Come here Marine.' And she went on walking towards the music room.

'What is happening? Last year even the Mother Inspector came to the playground to play a game of ping-pong with you. Do you think I didn't know? You were bright and happy, and full of enthusiasm. But now, Marine, I only see you hiding in corners with a faraway look in your eyes. You don't join in any longer. Why, Marine? What's the matter? Something disagreeable must have happened. You can trust me. Or at least find a person you trust and try to open yourself up.'

We went into the music room. Sister Nivalda looked deep into my eyes as if trying to discover the secret of my soul.

'No, Sister Nivalda, there is nothing wrong with me. I only miss my parents and brothers.'

'You know I don't believe you. You always missed your family. But you were never downhearted. You never had your head in the clouds.'

'It's only a passing mood. That's what I think, Sister.'

Not even I knew what was happening to me. And I had not noticed it, until Sister Nivalda pointed it out.

'Pray, my girl, that you will again become the person you were last year,' she said as she left me.

I went back with my head down, past the girls who were practising, without noticing them. When I got to the end of the long room, the notes of "Le lac de Como" followed me and flowed into my soul.

Sister Ita, our assistant, ordered me to take care of the library while the librarian Sister was busy with other things. The year before, I had helped in the Secretary's office, but as there was now a new Secretary, I was not needed, since there was not much to be done. I helped a little at the start of the year and then went to work in the library. I liked this because there I would get the chance to read, and reading has always been my favourite pastime.

Nostalgia, anguish and a feeling of loneliness gradually began to take hold of me. Only the reading of authors which girls of my age would never read helped me forget that strange inner moment that had destroyed that happy world of mine. I helped one of the girls with her research and went back to my Cronin book and was immersed in it when I was startled to hear Father Jonathan's voice outside the library window.

'What time will Confession start tomorrow?' he was asking someone.

'At 3 pm' replied a voice that I recognised as being that of Sister Alice.

'Tomorrow, just for the boarders?' said the priest.

'Yes, that's right.'

For no reason at all I started to tremble. That subject disturbed me. I closed the Cronin book and stood up. My head ached. My hands shook and my heart beat wildly. I leaned against the table and for the first time in my life I felt myself becoming a part of the bitter drama of life. I had already suffered a lot, but only at that moment something of the soul, something dramatic was happening to me, Marine, a second year High School pupil, poor and far from her family. But what was really happening? I asked myself. Nothing, I answered. I was an excellent pupil, esteemed by my colleagues and teachers, who always obeyed the school's rules and regulations... Might this be a case of masochism - suffering without knowing why?

The pupil, who had been reading in a corner of the room, returned her book and went out. The librarian, smelling of soap, came in and sat down, put her glasses on and said I could go. Then the bell rang for the end of study time and the start of prayers. Our rosary was prayed day at 5pm. It was followed by dinner and then by some time in the playground.

When I got to the chapel the girls were already there, kneeling and waiting for the sister to signal the start of the rosary.

'Will tomorrow's Mass be a Requiem, Sister Alice?', Father Jonathan's voice could be heard coming from the sacristy. A cold shiver went through my whole body, from head to foot, and before I got to my place in the chapel, I heard Sister Alice answering:

'Yes, Father Jonathan, everything is ready.

I knelt down. One last ray of sun shone through the multicoloured chapel window. The lilies on the altar reminded me of purity, and their scent calmed my soul.

I prayed silently: 'Holy Virgin, don't ever abandon me. Each person is a mystery and I am so complicated! Give me courage to face myself!'

Silent tears rolled down my cheeks and dropped on the cold floor, between the benches. I didn't know what was happening but I felt abandoned and without an aim in life.

The prayers soon ended but I did not even say a Hail Mary.

On leaving the Chapel we met the Chaplain outside the Sacristy. He had a word with each of us, stopping some and chatting longer with them. My colleagues were used to his easy-going informality, but deep inside they all despised him and when possible would whisper and laugh behind his back.

After dinner and playtime, night came and the stars were

already shining in the clear sky. The chattering of the pupils contrasted with the serenity of the beginning of night. In the clear sky one or two birds reminded me of my childhood in my homeland.

I stopped at the front door of the main building and looked around. The old walls, with their many black stains caused by time and nature, seemed hostile. The large old windows, bare of paint, gave the impression of being witches' teeth set in a diabolical smile... Over the old roof, the large palm trees of the yard peeped at me silently, as if someone much higher up and with wide open eyes was watching me in a sinister way...

I remembered Sister Nivalda's words:

'You don't join in any longer ...'

I ran my hands over my face, rubbing my eyes, trying to push away that hostile vision of the old school building.

I tried to talk to the girls in my class. But I gave up and withdrew into my shell. I could not 'join in'. Why not? There was no good reason. I just didn't. What's more, I did not know what was happening to me inside. Sometimes an anguish would torture my soul; at others an intimate desire to possess something or to be possessed by something unknown... The feeling of being a casualty of the universe, a desire to suffer more and more... To enter the strange world of nostalgia and the bizarre – the world of nothing.

Silent tears rolled down my cheeks, changing that happy face that had always been mine. Faith, pity, prayers - everything was going astray, and only an open sore – myself - throbbed and bled without being helped...

I ran my hand through my hair. It was long and silky but

I had lost my feminine vanity. I was close to collapse and spiritual extinction.

I heard the bell and went with the others to the classroom. There I felt protected and safe from danger. I was glad to see we were to have a Portuguese language test. This cheered me up as I felt the urge to study and to be Someone (with a capital S) had returned, and it would never leave me, even if this meant a great sacrifice.

When I opened the Portuguese book, I saw a small piece of paper written with a pencil. Then I read:

'In our lives, we often come across a tree which hides a forest from our eyes.' (Michael Quoist).

I read it again, trying to analyse the words of the famous Michael Quoist, in relation to what was happening to me.

Could there be anything worse?

The tree might represent my anxiety. And the forest? What would be the meaning of the forest in the large context of my soul? The forest... I thought. Only time can tell...

I did very well in the Portuguese exam. Sister Antônia was an excellent teacher and we could feel her evangelising spirit even during grammar and literature classes. She wanted our literary formation to be complete. Culture, information and intelligence would be of little value if they were not accompanied by a change for the better in behaviour.

Our religious formation was very rigid and even in 1968, a year of great educational and social changes, Religious Doctrine was a compulsory subject in the curriculum.

We had everything we needed: the right environment to

grow up free of outside difficulties, guidance on the part of the Sisters during the whole day and rigorous teaching.

At that time young people were compliant, accepting theological teachings with faith and no arguments. The Roman Catholic doctrine (we would never change our religion!), was supreme and infallible, showing us Heaven and Hell, already transformed into "states of soul" and not as places where devils and angels awaited the "Blessed and Damned of the Father".

Yet everything was changing. God was becoming less severe. The teachers of religions were coming to accept that heaven and hell are states of the soul and not places under and above the Earth as they used to think - with fire and brimstone or angels singing among the sparkling stars. There were wrongs to be righted: it was time tell children the truth.

From then on the Church started to recognise that it had been too strict in the past, and had to be influenced by these new times. Wasn't Pope Paul VI an existentialist? Was Vatican Council II just a meeting of top ecclesiastics?

The Papal Encyclicals were carefully studied by all of us. Our doubts were few, and the Sisters immediately tried to clear them.

As for myself, 1968 was a year of dark inner conflict. Apart from the unexplained anguish that I was suffering, the study of some philosophical works started to shake my ideas and things, which I considered unique, infallible and immutable. Plato's teachings inspired me even though many people thought they were absurd. The philosophy teacher only talked about the subject without revealing her own point of view. And we reacted to each new theory feeling that now everything was really explained at last.

As for religion, there was a word very much in fashion at that time which we liked. It was "engagement". The Christian should always be "engaged" I was a young dynamic Catholic but deep down I was always questioning, trying to explore those certain truths which could not be explained, the "dogmas". Yet there are no explanations for dogmas, and it was because of them that I often missed daily communion. I wanted to understand before I joined in.

My diary has some interesting reflections on the spiritual climate of the 1960s such as "Faith is adhering to Christ. And to the Church."

At that time, even in the midst of doubts, we just rose above them because true faith meant blind belief, belief without asking questions as the Church insists. "Faith is adherence to Christ. If you don't believe you can't belong".

It was not difficult to belong to the Church. You believed and that was that. There is more questioning now. Modern people prefer a faith which can stand up to questioning. They prefer to study, research and evolve, knowing that they believe because they understand. They worship because they understand and believe. The light is no longer hidden under the bushel.

At 1 pm a notice was put on the board. "Confessions will be heard today beginning at 3 pm".

I read the notice. I sat down and felt perplexed. I didn't know if I should go to confession or not. Why, my Lord? I always confessed weekly and communed daily. What was the reason for such a change?

'I am going to the Library, Sister Ita, because the librarian left the keys with me.' I said cheerfully, knowing that there would be no time to confess.

'Yes, Marine. There will be plenty for you to do there.'

Many pupils were waiting outside the library door. As soon as I opened it, they went in looking for the front seats. As soon as all had been seen to and had found what they were looking for, I sat down and started my work without being interrupted.

At 2.30 pm we heard a voice coming from the yard. It was Father Jonathan arriving.

'What silence', he said to Sister. 'It doesn't seem as if so many girls live here!'

'Yes, they are hard at work.'

'Haven't they come down yet?'

'Not yet. I'll tell them you're waiting in the Confessional.'

Even if I wished I could not have got near the Confession sacrament. I was in charge of the Library and this made me feel happy and relieved.

The girls went to the Chapel in groups of six, and when the bell rang to end the study period, the priest was still hearing confessions.

I locked the Library and went to the Chapel after the Rosary had started. I went in and tried to pretend that I did not know that Father Jonathan was still in the Confessional.

* * *

Our dormitory was very large with numerous windows, which opened to the inner yard. On the hottest nights, the windows of the dormitory were left open. As I suffered from lack of air, my bed was always close to one of them.

I should explain what I meant by this. I once asked Sister Ita:

'I would like to sleep close to the window, because I feel a lot of lack of air at night if you don't mind. I would be very grateful.'

'Of course you can put your bed close to the window, Marine! And, if you feel this lack of air, you need to go to the doctor; at your age it is not right. When did it begin?'

'It is not exactly a lack of air, Sister. It began when I was at school in Belo Horizonte. I was taking a shower, when, suddenly, something took over my body, a strange thing suffocating me, making me feel dizzy. It seemed that my body was becoming too big, the arms and the fingers disproportional, everything being thick and enormous. I went to the doctor and he said that I was fine, that there was nothing wrong, nothing at all.

'Since then I've often felt these strange symptoms and sometimes, I even feel that I am not me. Sometimes I even think I must be dying.'

'Marine, tomorrow we will take you to the doctor. Don't worry, you'll find it's not serious.'

There may have been nothing physically wrong with me, yet I continued to feel that there were times when I was not me. Sometimes, at night, I would find myself in a strange house, like a luxurious palace, where there was something very unpleasant going on – I couldn't understand exactly what, but I clearly remember a very strange-looking and very white man who was somehow involved.

I had never been anywhere like this as a child, nor could I remember reading about it in a book. This was real. I was the grown-up lady who lived in that beautiful room. Then the memory would fade, and at last I was able to get to sleep.

On Sunday mornings we used to listen to music and play games, or go for a stroll around the square in front of our school. On one occasion I was so absorbed in my thoughts that I did not notice Father Jonathan until he snapped his fingers in front of my eyes and exclaimed 'Come back to the real world!'

'Father Jonathan! I didn't know you would be around!'

'What were you thinking about, Marine?'

'Then you know my name?'

'Why shouldn't I know it?'

He smiled, and looked into my eyes as if he was searching for something.

'How are you doing in school?'

'Well. Do you know what class I'm in?'

'Second year'.

'How do you know, if we never spoken to each other before?'

'I don't know how... Why don't you ever confess, Marine?'

'Oh really, Father! Then you know who goes and who doesn't go to Confession?'

'Why, Marine?' he asked me softly and tenderly.

'Sometimes I want to go, but I lose my nerve when the time comes.'

'Has it always been like this?'

'No, only this year, 1968. A year of bad luck.'

'Why bad luck?'

'I don't know, Father Jonathan, but I miss last year. I used to look at life with more optimism, with more enthusiasm...'

'And why did you lose your enthusiasm?'

'It seems as if the pain and suffering of the whole world suddenly took hold of me.'

'Don't say such things, you sound like a grumpy old woman!'

'Maybe, but it's the truth.'

'I hope to see you in the Confessional on Thursday,' he said as he turned to leave. I promised to do my best.

A couple of weeks later I came across Father Jonathan in the passage outside my classroom.

'You didn't go,' he said.

'Go where?'

'To Confession.'

'I will go, but I don't think I've committed any serious sins lately,' I said playfully as I went into the classroom.

'Hey, what's the hurry?'

'An important class, Father. I can't miss it. We'll talk some other time.'

'Of course. Off you go, then!'

The name 'Jacques Maritain' was written on the blackboard. 'Who's he?, I asked my classmate Edilene.

'I've no idea. I hate philosophy.'

The teacher dictated: 'Maritain is a French philosopher, born in Paris in 1882. He was a pupil of Bergson who, in the name of Catholic orthodoxy and the new scholasticism, opposed his professor's way of thinking. Far from orthodox, he sought to unite various aspects of reality such as the Freudian unconscious, the Jungian collective archetype of humanity, the rituals of the magic of technologically backward peoples. He maintained that Christians were morally committed to social justice.'

After the dictation the teacher asked if there were any questions.

'Who was Jung, and what are collective archetypes?' somebody asked.

'Carl Gustav Jung was a Swiss psychiatrist and analyst. He was a follower and a collaborator of Freud, but later on parted company with him. To Jung, archetypes are eternal ideas that serve as models. He sees man as a collective being. He represents his species and after he dies he will return to join the world of the archetypes (or ideas) where all will become united, forming a collective.

'Seems like an oriental theory of reincarnation,' I said quietly.

'What did you say, Marine?', asked the Sister with a smile.

'I said Jung's theory was like the eastern reincarnation theory.'

'It is. You are right. There is something in common between Jung, Plato and the reincarnationist theories.'

'That's interesting, Sister. If during one's lifetime we remember things that are in the world of ideas, as Plato said, it is because we have lived before!'

'Marine!', said the teacher crossly. 'Let's return to Maritain, shall we?' Everyone laughed.

I no longer paid attention to Maritain. That remark about Jung excited me as had the class on Plato the month before.

Why do I keep remembering things if I didn't live them? That is, I didn't live them here, after I was born. Oh Lord! What a mystery! That magnificent castle or palace... Such a clear moon... that white and repugnant person trying to impose... Again, on a clear Monday morning, during a class on philosophy, I was remembering... No! It wasn't fair to suffer this way for something so strange! But it didn't depend on me. It was a distant memory, but a real one.

'Socrates... Plato... Jung... Interesting, Maritain is a Catholic and seeks to cooperate with theories the Church does not accept'.

The following day I went to the Chapel to confess. Several colleagues, including Edilene, were already there. Hiding her mouth with the veil, she said softly:

'Marine, this is my first confession this year, and tomorrow will be my first communion this year.'

'Why? You always confessed and took communion!'

'Do you remember what I promised to tell you?'

'Yes. What is it?'

'Do you remember the story I told you last year, about the priest in my home town who was caught kissing a girl?'

'Yes, I remember, but what has that to do with your keeping away from Holy Communion?'

'Marine! You still don't understand. The priest was Father Jonathan! He comes from my home town. He was the priest there before he moved to São Paulo.'

I had a moment of panic, then I replied hesitantly:

'Edilene, I don't think one mistake justifies another. The priest is a man like all others and he can fall down like anybody else. What's more important is that he is authorised to be a Minister of Christ. Didn't Peter, the first head of the Church, go astray? And he was chosen directly by Christ himself. Priests make mistakes because they are human but the Church will endure! We have to play our part!'

'Yesterday, Marine, I talked with Sister Ita and told her everything. She advised me to come to Confession today. She said practically everything you said. I feel better, and I'm going to try, but only God knows how difficult it is.'

'Edilene, this is also the first time I have come to confess with Father Jonathan.'

'Then you haven't confessed this year?'

'Yes I have, but with the Sister's confessor.'

'And why not with Father Jonathan?'

'I don't know. I hadn't courage. Father Jonathan frightens me but I don't know why...'

'My goodness, Marine!' said my friend, making the sign of the cross.

Edilene went after the last girl left the Confessional. She took about ten minutes. Then it was my turn. I knelt down and made the sign of the cross. The priest pulled the curtain back a bit and said:

'You made up your mind at last!' My palms began to sweat.

'Why do you only take Holy Communion now and then? You stay away for a couple of days then you come back again'

'Sometimes I lose my faith. Everything seems worthless and pointless. Why take Holy Communion?'

'And why do you feel it is worthless and pointless?'

'I believe in Christ, but the Church...'

'The Church?'

'Yes, Father. The Church doesn't explain what it preaches!'

Father Jonathan laughed. 'You are funny, Marine'

I felt rather offended and almost wished I had not come to confession.

'You must be referring to the "dogmas". The essentials are there, the values of our Faith. Don't be a doubting Thomas, Marine. Blessed are those who have not seen but still believe'

'But it doesn't depend on me. I believe everyone loses their faith sometimes.'

'Yes, Marine, especially young people seeking for self-assertion. But don't give up!'

'Yes, Father. That's right.'

'Are you doing well in school?'

'Yes, thank God! I love studying.'

'Do you have a boyfriend?'

I shuddered. I didn't know if I had one or not. Didn't Marcinho tell me, the second time we met, that he was going to marry someone else? My hope was still alive. I always liked him. He had married and became a widower soon afterwards. And now that I had met him again, he had someone else!

I shook off those dark thoughts and replied:

'There is someone I like, but he has another girl friend.'

'Get another one. You can't go on suffering because of someone who doesn't care for you.

'Here in school, even if one has a boyfriend, it is as if you don't have one. I live a long away from here and only my family concerns me.'

'Where do you live?'

'In J. S.'

'And why don't you study there?'

'There is no boarding school there,' I said, trying to get away from my own thoughts.

'Marine, I'm glad you came. Come always to Confession. Christ forgives us in the peace of Christianity, and it is through a priest that we receive useful advice. Don't let the problem of faith worry you.'

I left and went to pray, kneeling on the last bench. The Chapel was empty. The lilies, which always pleased me, were on the altar. The same afternoon sun shone on the walls through the stained-glass windows. I remembered what Edilene had told me, what I had replied, and what Father Jonathan had said to me.

People should get together and help each other, I thought. Why throw stones? Why can't a priest err? And why can't he marry? It would be better. Man's heart was made to love and priests have a heart beating in their breast like all other men.

On the way out, Father Jonathan was waiting for me in a small corridor at the end of the chapel. His small eyes were shining. That curly hair that irritated the "upper class" was getting white. In spite of his happy expression his face showed that he had suffered in his time.

Poverty did indeed have a positive side. It taught me to become friendly with a girl suffering from epilepsy (when everyone nearly withdrew, afraid of her convulsive fits); with a deaf girl who hid her wealth behind her humility; and with a dark-skinned priest with curly black hair, whose family lived by begging in his hometown...

I remembered Edilene's story when I saw Father Jonathan. Poor Father Jonathan! Being criticised by an empty-headed girl, full of prejudice!

'Are you going to celebrate Mass to Our Lady tomorrow?' I asked him as I removed my veil.

'Yes. Are you going to take communion?'

'Of course'

The May 24th mass was celebrated every year in front of an enormous white image of Our Lady in the main courtyard. That afternoon it was like a silent desert. As we strolled across it, I asked:

'So you were living in São Paulo?'

'I stayed there for many years. I left many friends and a Parish to which I was devoted.'

'And why did you come here?'

'Vow of obedience, Marine. I am a priest. I can't forget that.' He seemed to be talking to himself.

'And why did you go to a Parish?'

'It needed a vicar...'

'And can a Priest of Congregation live in another Parish?'

'Yes.'

'Would you rather live in the College or in the Parish, on your own?'

'There is more to do in the Parish. Less time for empty thoughts.'

'You are right. Life in the College inspires romance. I want to write a book, Father Jonathan. Can you believe it? A book.'

We were near the boarders' dining room. Looking hard at me, he smiled and said:

'Put a sentence about the "Priest" in it.'

Our Lady's Day started well, happy and busy. Mass would

be at 4 pm, with several celebrating priests, a choir and many people from the city of N. P. After Mass there would be the traditional crowning of Our Lady.

After lunch, many pupils and teachers went to the courtyard in order to prepare the altar on the stand and decorate it. At 4:15 pm, wearing festive uniforms, new shoes and veils we took our places in front of the people who filled the courtyard. At 4:30 pm, Sister Fernanda, our philosophy teacher, called for silence and read from the pulpit:

'Then a great sign appeared in the sky. A woman dressed as the sun with the moon beneath her feet and a crown with twelve stars on her head...'

I slept well that night, but for Father Jonathan the night was not a calm one. Turning from side to side in his bed, he could still not understand why he had moved to that school in N.P.

It was awful leaving the large parish in M.R. that he liked so much. What use would he be cooped up, acting only as chaplain to those nuns and school girls full of prejudice? His things, the people he liked, his apostleship, his world were all in the parish of M.R. Why did God act in this way?

What he did in the huge parish of M.R. was the work of a true apostle. There he was accepted, listened to and admired. He was always with the people. He lifted the drunkard who was lying in the gutter, he offered his arm and a friendly cup of coffee. He carried the baby for a mother who had gone shopping, and had her hands full of bags and packages. He sat down with washerwomen as they were washing clothes, and chatted with them humbly and happily. Rich and poor were the same to him. He wandered through the slums and red light areas, where material and moral misery were two tumours sickening and shaming people of a higher social level.

Father Jonathan accepted his transfer to the school of his Congregation in N.P. with humility. But things now seemed to be building up inside him and he could not understand why God brought him from M.R. and his apostleship and put him in that school with practically nothing to do.

The priest turned around in his bed, pushing a tear with the back of his hand. He was not against the Holy Will of God. He only wanted a convincing explanation for to that change.

I had a little notebook in which I used to write my private thoughts. Due to the abrupt changes that were happening inside me, I started to write more frequently. At the end of May, when we went into the courtyard to say the rosary, I left the notebook on the shelf where I kept my veil and prayer books. The shelf had several small drawers, each one with the number of the pupil who used it. Mine was 7. The next day, when I went to get the veil for Mass, I couldn't find my notebook.

I felt a pain in my chest and a cold sweat on my hands. The notes I had made were not against school regulations, nor had they anything to do with the Sisters. There was nothing immoral in it, just my private thoughts. So personal that it was unthinkable that anyone else should read them

I was worried during and after Mass, so I asked Sister Alice, who worked in the Sacristy, if she had found it. She had not. I asked my best friends, but no one had seen it.

'It must have been found by one of the Sisters,' said Edilene.

For the rest of the day I could hardly concentrate on my work

During the day, I was hardly able to do my homework and, in the Library, I felt so dizzy I was unable to find a book. When it was time to say the rosary, I was one of the first to get to the shelf and get my veil. Much to my surprise I found the notebook on top of the prayer book. The sight of a piece of paper inside the notebook and some pencil marks on the pages stopped my sigh of relief. There was something written on it, but I did not read it. I folded it up and went into the Chapel. After the service, I unfolded it and found the words 'Marine, I have to talk to you. In the confessional, OK? Father Jonathan.'

Seeing that I looked worried and angry, Edilene came up to me.

'Well, Marine, did anything happen?'

'No!' I almost shouted.

'Do you already know who picked it up?'

'No. I couldn't find out. Excuse me, Edilene. I'm going to put it away. I'll be back soon.'

When I returned, Edilene was leaning against the handrail of the staircase that leads to the yard.

'Are you feeling better now?'

'Yes.' I replied.

'Marine, I am taking communion daily. Did you notice?'

'Yes. Edilene, please tell me more about Father Jonathan. What is his family like?'

'He comes from a very poor family. His mother is a washerwoman; he has no father and his only sister is a woodcutter. They used to beg. There is also a brother called Fernando.'

'So, he is despised for two reasons: for his colour and because of his poverty.'

'You may have noticed that he doesn't care.'

'People who are spiritually evolved ignore such things, Edilene, although they feel them deep in themselves.'

It was only later that I studied Father Jonathan's pencilled comments.

On one page I had written "The most important thing is to be with Christ and practice Charity. The Church only complicates things."

In the margin Father Jonathan had written "The first part is nice, but don't speak ill of the Church."

Further on I wrote: "I went to confession today. I trembled. I don't know why, but Father Jonathan exerts a strong influence over me. I like him. He is a kind of good and humble priest but I can't explain why.... I'd rather not be near him..."

At the side Father Jonathan wrote: "I want an explanation."

My latest entry was:

"I am the leader of the group which is going to hand in the work 'Eurico, the Presbyterian' by Alexandre Herculano. It will be the most important debate of the College! It will be against priestly celibacy. We will show its disadvantages by criticising the Church that created it.

In his introduction, Alexandre Herculano says: "In my opinion, as a weak contender, I have only thought of celibacy as a feeling, and I have always felt, with respect to the solitude to which the Church condemns its ministers, a kind of spiritual amputation, in which in the priest there dies the hope of completing his life on Earth. Think about all the joys and all consolations that heavenly images and living faith may generate, and you will find these don't compensate for the sorrow of one's solitude. Without women the world becomes a melancholy wilderness.

"Our group will analyse priesthood through the ages. The essential in human being is the Soul, yes, but God gave this Soul a fleshly body. Why condemn human affection and sex? God help me! Our work must be great!"

Father Jonathan had scribbled in the margin:

"Be careful, Marine, not everyone is sufficiently mature to understand what you are trying to explain."

I put the notebook away and rested my head on the desk. My head whirled. Father Jonathan could never get to know my way of thinking, my feelings, my activities. It would be hard to speak to him now. My world was falling apart faster than I could have imagined. Father Jonathan knowing my secrets! It was totally absurd!

I couldn't sleep that night and didn't take communion the next day. When I went to confession in the afternoon, I felt dominated, as if I was in Father Jonathan's hands. This terrified me.

'Father! For the love of God tell me how you discovered my notebook. You didn't have the right to... Please, don't misunderstand me. I don't want you to feel hurt, but the notebook is mine! They are my feelings, they are not sins but just my own feelings!'

'Marine! Calm down, please! I saw when you put the notebook there; it fell down and I picked it up to put it back. As it was open I started to read a few words and ended by keeping it because I felt it was my duty to talk with you.'

'Do you feel that what I wrote is very serious?'

'Look! I think your ideas are very advanced but I confess that I agree with you. I think so too!'

'What? You wrote that I should not attack the Church.'

'I was referring to the work you're going to hand in on Herculano's book.'

'Do you think I should?'

'You must be careful! It's a very delicate subject and you might shock many people.'

'We are going to stir things up at school.'

'Why do you feel a priest should marry?'

'For two reasons: the first one is because the priesthood does not make it impossible for the priest to have a family. The second is that the priest is human and like all humans, with a heart to love and be loved. Why suffer and worse, often do what is forbidden, causing scandals?'

'Do you feel it is scandalous for a priest to be fond of someone?'

'No, but the Church does not allow it.'

'Why did you write that I exert a strong influence over you? Are you, by any chance afraid of me?'

'No, it's not fear, but I can't explain it... I'm going to leave Father. I feel the confession box is being profaned.'

'Not at all. You are going through a series of difficulties and I am here to help you. Marine, suffering, doubts and dilemmas are made for us. We have to be brave. Believe me, I want to help you.

'It's only a book that is getting me excited, that's all.'

'Try to give your opinion by all means, but be careful. Don't exaggerate.

'Don't jump to conclusions without careful analysis.'

'Yes, Father. I'll do what I can.'

'Could I ask you a favour? Show me your Diary now and then.'

'I'm not going to write anything else.'

'Yes you are. And I want to see it.'

'Why, Father Jonathan?'

'Life is not what people think it is. Life is something very natural. We complicate everything.'

I felt dizzy and went out to the yard, where the other girls were. Dinner was a bit late so we went on talking near the dining room.

'What's happening? asked Edilene in a low voice.

'Nothing. Why?'

'You are pale!'

'I took some funny medicine today.'

'What medicine?'

'I don't know, Edilene,' I said as I walked away.

Two days later on a cold and quiet afternoon I was doing some homework when someone outside the window said "psiu". I raised my head and saw Father Jonathan at the window.

'How's the Portuguese work doing?

'Well. The great day is near. We are only waiting for the group of Camilo Castelo Branco to finish the presentation of "The Love of Perdition".

'I would like to see it,' he said with a smile.

I got up and went to the window. Father Jonathan enchanted me with his simplicity and greatness. Spiritual greatness. A spirit purified by what the flesh suffered.

'Marine, I'm a kind of Eurico.'

'You mean the humble priest in the book "Cartéia"? Do you identify yourself with him?'

'Marine, it's all so sad. You end up all on your own. I trust you, don't get me wrong.'

'Of course, Father. Now I have a strong reason for my argument: I know someone who suffers from "spiritual amputation".'

'Can I trust you?'

'Of course, Father, even if I can't be of any use. I also need someone very much.'

'You can count on me; we'll be friends.'

'Thank you, Father Jonathan.'

'Not Jonathan - Eurico!'

'Eurico is an ugly name, Father. In honour of Alexandre Herculano you will now be "Alexandre".'

Father Jonathan laughed and then, in a sad voice, repeated

'Alexandre...'

Outside, the trucks passed by, carrying the labourers coming back, shaking with cold, from the coffee and sugar cane plantations.

I looked towards the road and repeated one of the many ironic sayings of Alexandre Herculano:

"Man is no doubt strong and the finest work of Creation. Glory to the King of Nature that groans as it shivers."

'Many people suffer in this town, Marine. Those who work most receive less.'

'There is a great divide here,' I said. 'Only rich and poor people. Nothing in between.'

'You can't imagine the poverty up the hill. I celebrate Mass there on Sundays and it would be so good if you could come with me sometimes, so we could do some work together, trying to improve the lives of those people.'

But we didn't. We lived a selfish life. We didn't know what was happening in the world, in Brazil or even around us. Not knowing the troubles of the world we were not prepared to face them and life with its problems... We were so dependent, undecided, submissive, naive... Everything was too easy.

I said good-bye and closed the window. All night long I thought of the Portuguese lesson and what Father Jonathan had said. I thought of the wretched lives of the people coming back from the sugar and coffee plantations, of the sad reality of a person who would like to be somebody but whose financial condition was nonexistent. Would I tell Father Jonathan, that is, Alexandre, things about my life?

Cold dawn arrived. And reality slowly disappeared. Father Jonathan's image faded, and at the same time my body seemed large, horrible, strange, and breathing became difficult. Suddenly, I felt the presence of someone mysteriously white and incomprehensible, looking half crazy. Incomplete images appeared and disappeared in my mind leaving an agonising vacuum... Those were painful moments that I didn't reveal to anyone because I did not know how to describe them.

Next day Father Jonathan was at the school. He asked me to write down in my Diary my latest impressions. He could not have known that it was full of notes. And my suffering and the need to continue writing increased as I wrote.

In the evening study time, I wrote on a piece of paper:

"Alexandre, I have faced many inner difficulties. I can't explain what is happening to me. Why does God act this way with us? Pray for me at the altar. Marine."

Next day on entering the chapel I placed the paper in his hands.

The days went by slowly as did my immense inner anguish. The nights were long and terrible, mostly awake, trying to find out the reason for living, for suffering, for searching...

The great day was at last about to arrive! The day before, sister Antônia tried to find out why the second year class was so excited. Somebody told her it was because Marine's group was going to hand in their work on Eurico the Presbyterian and it would be a lively day because Marine's group was going to discuss he question of celibacy for priests, making it clear that they are against it.

Sister Antônia was very cross. She sent for me and cancelled the presentation until we changed our opinions.

I said: 'Sister Antônia, it is just a debate. My group will give its point of view while you and another group will contest it. That should be interesting, Sister. Two groups discussing priestly celibacy, each giving its point of view!'

'No, Marine! Either you present your work without including your absurd ideas or I will cancel your group's presentation.'

'All right, Sister. I'll think about it and give you an answer later.'

Sister Antônia smiled. I know that deep down she admired my desire to win, my strong temperament and my frankness. I liked her way of speaking, her gentle way of correcting people, especially me, and her religiosity. We were always good friends.

In the afternoon I told Father Jonathan what had happened.

'Didn't I say so? Here in this school they are not ready for your kind of presentation.'

'But, Father...'

'No, Alexandre.'

'But, Alexandre, the group would give its opinion. Then the others and the teacher would counter and give their points of view.

'Would you like some advice? Emphasise the literary side, the style, the contents, the poetic language of the author, etc. and leave out the part about priestly celibacy'.

'It won't be easy. I think I'll just keep quiet.'

'I want to know what happened. Don't stop taking communion, Marine. There is no reason for you to stay away. I'm saying this as a priest and as a friend.'

During recess in the evening I sought Sister Antônia and told her I was ready to present my work, leaving out my way of thinking.

'You must feel sure that you made a mistake, Marine' said Sister Antônia. You are absolutely mistaken. The greatest value of priesthood and the religious life is the giving up of human love and pleasure, that are beautiful and blessed by God, but which we give up in favour of a wider and greater love.'

I looked at her pretending that I was convinced and humbly added:

'I need some time before class to tell my colleagues of the group about such changes.'

'That's fine, Marine! It's through our experiences, even the frustrating ones, that we climb the steps of life. It is not important to be right all the time, but to recognise that we make mistakes and that we are always ready to start again.'

I left quickly and paused under a palm tree in the inner courtyard. Sitting down there I could think about what was happening. I was like something weird, not of this world; things and people around me seemed strange and distant. I had lost my last chance to show my capacity for expanding and defending a subject.

That evening Father Jonathan went to his college library to look for Eurico the Presbyterian. He felt that only he should be aware of Marine's problems. And the biggest problem was the presentation of that work whose author had excited her, which discussed the solitude of priesthood.

Father Jonathan opened the book and started walking around the empty library.

"And who told you, priest, that your love was not a crime? Your conscience is right. When at the feet of the venerable Siseberto, the nobleman Eurico swore that he had abandoned the world, and would reject worldly passions.

"The light of his affections and hopes that shone and filled my heart with happiness had to go out, like the lamp of the temple at dawn; because I had turned to heaven and the light of the Lord. But the Sun just rose for me and soon disappeared, and those who believe I live in light can't imagine that I live in darkness!

"My passions could not die because they were large, and what is immense is eternal.

"And so, I dare not ask for the peace of death; because for me there will be no peace unless I am annihilated What did I do, my God, to only have inside me a happy thought, merely a desire large enough to fill the abyss of my unhappiness?

What harm did I do to cause this desire that condemned me to eternal anguish? But for me as for him, such thoughts are in vain. Oh Eternity, man's soul is buried and arrested in your boundless domain."

To himself, Father Jonathan said: 'Marine sees everything through the eyes of an adolescent. Sensitive souls don't read such words as those of Alexandre Herculano's with indifference. Especially young girls. Some day the schools will change and the pupils will be able to say what they think. Poor Marine, what will happen to you when this day comes? What will life have done to her simple and pure soul? And how about me? What will life have done to another sad and solitary Eurico?

'Today, Marine, I'm sure of one thing: the years that pass remind us more of our losses than our gains. And only the souls whose arrow is pointed upwards are granted a path which leads to God.

'The greatest loss is the physical separation caused by death. Tears fall; we feel remorse; we lament; all the times passed together are remembered with bitterness; memories fill the empty space in our heart... But if this heart believes in something beyond matter, everything will become easier.

'The transformation of the body, which many consider to be the end, will only benefit the spirit.'

The presentation of the work went ahead. My colleagues spoke about the plot; and I spoke about the style and life of the author.

When the talk was over, we offered to answer questions from the class and teacher. Several colleagues participated questioning the work. Priestly celibacy, loneliness, and the religious life of the Middle Ages were discussed, but not by me.

At the end, we were applauded, and got ten out of ten. Our work was the best one, but for me something was missing. We had not mentioned that detail that no one dared to discuss. And when someone wanted to speak about it, she was severely threatened.

I was relieved that it was over. It was another victory, though I felt as if I had lost. Holidays were coming. I was happy because I would be seeing my family and staying with them for a few days. The problems of a schoolgirl in crisis would be set aside. The routine which made life so monotonous would be abandoned. The joy of going back to J. S., of seeing its narrow streets and colonial churches, its railway station and old fashioned engine... The joy of seeing all this was like pure oxygen entering my breast, making me smile. A smile which disappeared when a voice outside the classroom called my name.

Father Jonathan was in the corridor and as soon as I left the classroom he asked me about the presentation.

'I did what you advised me to do. We got top marks.'

'Well done! Someday everything will change, Marine. Schools will be different, and pupils will be able to express their opinions without fear'.

Sister Antônia came up and embraced me warmly.

'Congratulations, Marine. Your work was excellent.' And turning to the priest she said: 'Father Jonathan, I wish all my pupils liked literature as much!'

'Marine is going to write a book,' said Father Jonathan.

'And I think she has already started it.'

'No, I haven't. I have only written a few poems. But I'll get there.'

'Our Marine is a bit of a pessimist,' said Sister Antônia. 'But she writes very well.'

Term was over. I took the bus to J.S. and walked to my grandmother's house, I went home early the next day.

My first surprise during the holidays was a lovely card from Father Jonathan. I was both happy and sad because I thought that during the holidays I would get rid, at least in part, of the anguish of liking Father Jonathan and having a heavy conscience.

The card had been posted the day I left. This is what he wrote:

"Marine, your absence is terrible. The school has lost its charm and I don't know how I'm going to spend the long days. Please write, so we may be together even when far away. What were the trip and the holidays like? Here it rained on the afternoon of the 29th. Seemed on purpose... Answer me, please! I'll stop now and wait for your long letter. Alexandre."

A week later I received another letter from Alexandre. It was a bulky envelope with cards, a long letter full of news and complaints, such as "The school without pupils is like a cage without a bird." He wrote about loneliness, boredom and the emptiness of vacations.

During July we exchanged letters frequently. I had no time to think of going out and enjoying myself. I had my problems and not even my holidays solved them. Distance strengthened that affection between a priest and a young girl, lonely and unsure of herself.

Family problems didn't bother me so much. I hardly noticed them, because mine were larger. I didn't think of going to S.N. to see Marcinho. He had someone else and it would have been a waste of time to look him up.

One afternoon my aunt came to see me with one aim in view: to give me some advice. 'Take care, Marine. I'm worried, my dear. Forget Marcinho. He is with someone else and is going to marry her. When he met you, his wedding day was already set.'

'Don't worry, Aunt Bianca. I'm going back to N. P. the day after tomorrow. Holidays are over and I'm going back. As for Marcinho, I no longer think about him.'

My aunt didn't believe me and she was right. I hadn't forgotten Marcinho, even during the most difficult moments in N. P. Even if he got married, I would always think of him with tenderness. Even when I was very young, he was always in my thoughts and such an old and deep sentiment would not die easily.

In my youth Father Jonathan was a digression, a parenthesis containing few words but very meaningful ones. The explanation would come later in life, forming a complete and deeply existential story.

When I noticed that Father Jonathan liked me and I liked him, I began feel guilty, although there was nothing in our relationship that could be condemned. I just liked him and he liked me.

The education I had been given since I was twelve, when

I became a boarder, was extremely strict. The idea of liking, let alone loving, a man was considered to be shameful, even sinful, although my relationship with Father Jonathan was so pure that it could not be considered sinful at all. The things we had in common – that need to find and give support, that insecurity, and above all that tenderness that flowed from Alexandre's eyes – were the same as those that filled my heart with a boundless desire to give.

We exchanged letters regularly, and I began to feel like the guilty party. If Father Jonathan was making a mistake, or worse, I was afraid he might go to Hell one day just because he liked me.

One day I learned that the school was no longer to accept boarders.

That meant I had to leave, and that meant saying good-bye to Father Jonathan. As I tried to do so, I began to cry and the words stuck in my throat.

'Don't cry Marine,' he said. 'This is life. Saying good bye is sad. I know we are going to suffer. We are going to miss each other but we have to be strong. I'll pray for you and I know you'll pray for me. You're young and I'm sure you'll be very happy. Some day, who knows? We might meet... Perhaps I'll go to J. S... Now off you go. Regards to your people. Cheer up, Marine. Everything we're going through was planned for us. Life is beautiful thanks to such meetings and farewells. One day we'll see each other... God be with you, Marine. Don't forget me...'

I looked at Father Jonathan, my eyes filled with tears... my hand on my mouth to stop all sounds... I couldn't say a single word.

'I'll expect a letter from you,' said Alexandre quietly.

I nodded, promising to write, and turned away in a hurry.

'Psiu!' said Father Jonathan.

I turned my head.

'Give me a hug.'

I embraced him and when I looked at his eyes I saw they too were full of tears.

'This is life, Marine.'

I managed to say 'I'll write to you, Alexandre.' as I left.

When I got to the gate I looked back. The old building seemed more melancholy; the large garden older, tired... each flower-bed drier... each tree, sadder...

I looked back once again. Father Jonathan was at the gate waving good bye.

That image of Alexandre in his grey suit would never be forgotten... He looked so smart wearing a suit! But in a cassock he gave the impression of being sad and reminded me of "Eurico"...

I felt dizzy, like someone who had just left hospital, or a lamb about to be slaughtered...

* * *

In January 1969 our small town suffered the greatest tragedy it had seen in its 300 years of existence. Five children from the same family went for a swim in the river. The eldest girl, who was engaged, was 24 years old. Two other sisters were 22 and 19, their brother was 15 and their little sister was eight. Suddenly, the youngest girl got into difficulties and seemed about to drown. The others rushed to help and managed to pull her to the river bank, but then all four were swept away by the strong current.

It was a dreadful blow not only for the family but also for all of us. Everyone liked the girls. They were lovely young people and everyone felt terrible about such a shocking event. Could this have been God's will?

Soon after the death of the four youngsters, a humble family with several children attracted everyone's attention. Three young girls of the same family suddenly fell ill, and started to speak and act as if they were the three drowned girls. They cried, sent messages to the family and the future bridegroom and showed signs of considerable distress.

Doctors were called, and the priest came along to bless them. As many people went in and out of the house of the girls suffering from "possession" as watched the search for the bodies in the river. Some said the girls just needed a good smack. Others said they merely wanted to be the centre of attention, while others believed that the spirits of the drowned girls "possessed" the three sisters, which the victims' family found extremely offensive.

It was a painful situation, and I just could not believe that the spirit of a dead person could enter the body of another person, I thought all that was ridiculous and took no further interest in the story. Eventually, life returned to normal, although those who had known the girls and had been so fond of them had their doubts and could not accept such a sudden loss.

PART TWO

It was a cold and silent night in May 1972. In the room next to the kitchen, a healthy 4-month-old baby named Kildary was asleep. He was my first child. I had married Marcinho in February 1971 and the baby had been born in January of the following year.

We lived a quiet life in S. N., where Marcinho had a shop and also taught at the local school. I also gave classes in Portuguese, English and Religion in High School, and taught in the elementary school as well. The salary paid by the High School was insignificant, and the state school would go eight months without paying us. Even so we had a decent life, all the better now that we had our son Kildary.

S. N. was founded in 1674 by pioneers who came from the city of São Paulo looking for emeralds. A beautiful black mountain lends an air of mystery to the small town. It is a mountain full of legends and apparitions, while the town is full of fascinating legends about ghosts and shadowy figures dragging their chains… It is a small place where I was born, and to where I returned after got married.

Let us get back to my kitchen on the night of May 31st, 1972. I was near the stove, preparing a feeding bottle for the baby, before he woke up and started crying.

Marcinho was in his shop talking with friends. It was usual for friends in S. N. to meet in shops after closing time. The only people in our house were Kildary, who was asleep, and me.

A black and white plastic curtain made of strings hung from the door that separated the kitchen from the sitting room. I had my back to it as I was by the cooker, when I distinctly heard Father Jonathan's voice calling my name. I turned round quickly and saw the curtain moving as if someone had passed through it.

Frightened, I turned the stove off and ran to the bedroom. I lay down and started to analyse the occurrence: Why did I turn round to greet Father Jonathan when I hadn't seen him for three years? Where was he now? Why did we lose touch with each other? What was keeping us apart?

The last I had heard from him was in July 1970, when he wrote to me telling about his apostleship in B.H.. Why hadn't I written to him?

I concluded that maybe the priest had not called to me after all. I had been rather light-headed since Kilden was born... When Marcinho came home, I told him what had happened and he said maybe I was just tired.

That night I dreamed that a huge bed of lilies separated myself from Father Jonathan who, from the other side, was stretching his immensely long arms toward me, trying to reach me. My hands also tried to touch his but couldn't. When I took a few steps trying to get to the other side, my feet sank in the mud. The enormous bed of lilies was on a swamp. Father Jonathan said: "Come on, it's better over here! Come with me, Marine! Everything out there is so sad..." And his arms grew tremendously in an effort to pull me.

I woke up. Thank God, it was only a dream, I thought. But I couldn't get to sleep again, thinking about the boarding school, the nuns, my classmates, the town of N.P. - and Father Jonathan.

Next day, June 1st 1972, was a holy day (Corpus Christi). Marcinho was going to close his shop so that we could follow the procession. Kildary and I were ready, waiting for him. I went to the shop to tell my husband it was time to close it. On my way back to the house, Marcinho called me. I turned round, but the voice I had heard was not Marcinho's but that of Father Jonathan.

I went inside. But I had hardly closed the door when Marcinho, who had been listening to a local radio station, went out to the street and called me. I went back to the shop.

'What was the name of that friend of yours, the priest?', he asked me as he switched off the radio.

'Father Jonathan.' I said.

'He has just died in hospital, in B.H. He had a car accident in Amazonina Avenue. He had a relapse yesterday and died today.'

It is not easy to describe what I felt at that moment. I only know that the knot in my throat could not hold back my bitter tears. I went into the room and wept bitterly. I had to cry and Marcinho had to forgive me! Cry for the loss of my best friend! Cry for the pain of loss, cry for the remorse for not having kept in touch with him. Oh Lord, why did you take him? He never got to know my home... my son... didn't even know I had got married!

Remorse was too much for me. I followed the procession and my prayers were tears that no one could understand.

The greatest pain was when the band played the eucharist music. Father Jonathan loved popular songs, bands and processions.

Time passed... Yet the pain caused by the loss of a loved one never dies. Time just shows that life continues, and that crying does not bring the dead back to life. But I never accepted Father Jonathan's death with resignation. I started to ask God to let him appear to me, if a soul really existed after death. I prayed every night in the hope that Father Jonathan would appear to me and say something to me.

In 1973 we moved to the town of Oliva and rented a small house in a nice street near the centre. At that time I was studying pedagogy at the University of L. Although I didn't like the subject very much, I felt I needed it, in order to do a better job in the field of education.

In 1974 the psychology teacher asked us to write an essay on any topic we liked related to psychology.

I went to J.S. to visit relatives, and while I was there I went into a bookshop and spotted a book called Parapsychology, by Robert Amadou. I bought it for my essay, and enjoyed the subject. Accounts of J. B. Rhine's and Charles Richet's experiments and the case of the Fox sisters, made me all the more interested in the subject, but only for academic reasons. I did not get involved in it, though I went on praying for Father Jonathan to appear. However, I only dreamed of him twice – unimportant dreams which I have forgotten.

In 1975 we moved house when our daughter Késsia was born. One night, when she was still tiny, I dreamt that Peri, the enormous dog that belonged to our neighbour, was trying to push the door of our bedroom open. My husband wanted to go to the kitchen, but couldn't because Peri was in the living room, near the bedroom door. At last, much against his will, Marcinho managed to get to the kitchen and open the door in order to allow the dog to leave. It was a tense situation, because Peri didn't want to leave our house and any threatening movement could be dangerous.

I was woken up by a noise on the other side of our bedroom door. I began to shiver, and asked Marcinho to go and see what was making it, but he just muttered something, turned over and went back to sleep. A short time later Marcinho got up to go to work. When he opened the door, he jumped back and closed it.

'Come and see what we've got here!', he said.

'Oh no, I don't dare,' I replied.

Then Marcinho opened the door and yelled:

'Peri! Get out.'

On hearing the name, I got up. No! It couldn't be! Another meaningful dream!

Marcinho picked up a stool to protect himself with, opened the kitchen door and carefully guided Peri out to the yard. Later on we were told that the dog was afraid of fireworks. The day before there had been a party nearby and as our kitchen door was open, the dog had got into our house and hidden himself in a small room no one used.

Our daughter Keila was born in 1977, after a pregnancy of eight months. She was healthy and plump.

If I stopped to analyse my life I might say it was going backwards. I taught for a couple of months in a school in Oliva, but there were so many disagreeable incidents that Marcinho decided I should no longer work away from home. But there was work for me from a local newspaper, which published my poems and stories. I had many friends, but something was missing, and I didn't know what was it.

In August 1979, I entered a competition for a local government job. As I took the test I asked Father Jonathan's soul to help me. I wanted the job - I couldn't stand being confined to my home. I was not born to be cooped up.

Something had to change in my life, but I didn't know what or how.

A few months later the exam results were published in a local paper, which a neighbour saw and showed me. I had been approved and got the first place. I was delighted, but not for long. I was pregnant. How could I work with another baby?

I had a Mass said for Father Jonathan's soul and went to the Mass. I had given up religious practices for quite a time, although I didn't know why. I always considered the Christian philosophy marvellous, but the Roman Catholic Church did not give me what I needed spiritually. I read what other sects had to say, but didn't like it. All that remained was my faith in God and my nightly prayers, which perhaps were said more out of habit than of piety.

I had definite ideas regarding the infinite and the spiritual, yet a bizarre memory tormented me. It would lead to days of introspection and anxiety.

It was a memory of a moon, a field of silver-coloured corn, beautiful horses and dogs, and an enchanted forest. Then I have a blurred vision of a huge stately home where I am tormented by a very white and very strange man. At the thought of this strange figure, I feel fear, repugnance, shame, attraction and submission... I couldn't account for this, however hard I tried.

I came to accept the fact that these memories came from my own mind. I had been getting them since my early childhood, and I am quite sure they are not things that I actually experienced. They are just part of my spiritual life and I can't explain them. Moonlight confused me even more. It would make me feel that I had lived somewhere else as a member of the nobility. I felt I had to remember more but just could not do so.

The new government agency was to be inaugurated in May 1980, the month the baby was due. We asked for a substitute for me when work started. It was impossible. Either I would take the job or the person who got the second place would take over, which is what happened.

* * *

At 12 pm on May 25th, 1980 my son Kilden Alexandre was born. It was a normal birth with little pain, the happiest birth of my life.

Kilden was thin, very thin. His hands were always cold. Because of this I always put him in a corner of my bed, so that I could hold and warm those little hands.

We then lived in a small house that Marcinho had bought in a new district with nice houses. We were happy. Kildary, eight years old, was an intelligent and well-behaved boy. We were proud of him. The teachers said he was a mature and responsible kid. Késsia was in kindergarten and was doing very well. Keila was only three, a little kitten full of fun. Kilden, the baby, was a quiet child and slept well. Sometimes, however, when he was asleep he started breathing quickly, making quite a noise. "He's just dreaming" I would think as I changed his position.

After Kilden's birth, there was an inexplicable change in our house. At 9 pm one evening I was sitting on my bed feeding the baby. There was a small nightstand between the bed and the wall. The other children were already asleep in the next room. Everything was quiet and I was looking at Kilden's face while he sucked away, with his eyes closed.

I suddenly heard several knocks coming from the nightstand, about a foot away from me. Frightened, I called to Kildary, who came running in. I asked him if he had heard anything and he said he heard loud knocks in my room. Trembling, I put the baby on the bed and stood up. My legs were shaking, so I asked Kildary if he could go to the kitchen and get me a glass of water.

As he was about to leave the room we heard what sounded like steps of many people running in from the kitchen. Then there was a loud noise, as if they were banging on the refrigerator, which was opposite our bedroom door, with their bare hands. Kildary screamed, moved away from the door, and fell into a chair.

The noise continued, coming towards my room, and then turned towards the bathroom, where it stopped. It sounded like several people holding on to each other, as if they playing at being a train. The noise was like that of several people running and jumping.

Kildary didn't want to talk about it. Neither did I. The two of us, holding on to each other and trembling, went to the other room, got the girls and put them in my bed. Kildary joined them, and there we stayed, the door remaining closed until Marcinho came home.

There was more of this kind of thing to come. One Saturday night at midnight, Marcinho and I were in the kitchen having a cup of coffee and chatting. During weekends he got in late from work. The house was tidy and silent. The children were asleep. Suddenly we heard loud knocks in the pantry next to the kitchen. I jumped to my feet and hurried over to Marcinho.

Then we heard the noises again, louder and clearer. Marcinho also heard them. At first the knocks seemed to come from near the cupboard. The second time it definitely came from the baby's play-pen.

We went into the pantry. Nothing. Everything was quiet and undisturbed.

On another occasion at 9:00 pm, we were already in bed except for Marcinho, who was still at work. I heard the sound of high heels outside my bedroom window, coming from the ramp leading up to the porch at the door.

Nobody called. Nobody knocked. The high-heeled footsteps came into my room, going from the dressing table to Kilden's cradle. I covered my head and called Kildary, who came quickly. Again I put them all in my bed and locked the door, waiting for Marcinho to arrive.

A few days later, again at 9 pm, I was lying down and Kilden was asleep, when suddenly I saw a figure near the cradle, a figure that soon vanished.

Once, we went to bed much earlier than usual, and as I was tired, I soon fell asleep. I woke up hearing Marcinho's car coming down our street and going into the garage. My husband then slammed the door of the car, closed the gate and went up towards the porch. I heard his keys rattling as he went to open the front door.

As usual, I then heard the noise of the key in the lock. I also heard Marcinho tap the door with his key, because there was another key in the lock on the other side of the door. I must have forgotten to remove it, I thought.

I got up quickly and opened the door, meaning to tell him that I was so sleepy that I forgot to take the key out. But there was nobody at the front door, the garage door was still open and there was no sign of Marcinho.

Frightened, I ran inside and closed the door. I looked at my watch. It was 9:10 pm I took the key out of the lock and went to my room, unable to understand what was happening.

Marcinho's greatest wish was to redecorate that house and extend it. There was plenty of land, and he wanted to build more houses to rent.

We did the building work, and our new house was large and comfortable and looked lovely. However, that was unimportant to me. The feeling of emptiness that I felt sometimes and those strange noises were bothering me more and more.

The noises that I heard during my sleepless nights in the distant past of my childhood, were understood by my parents to be due to fear. Things that happen to children who can't get to sleep... Just imagination...

But now? I was no longer a child, but the noises still went on. My sons heard them. Once my husband also heard them. My house is not haunted. Noises occur wherever I am. I'm not paranormal, but I feel something strange in me. I'm afraid I'm going crazy...

In October 1981, our daughter Kristine was born. Kilden was one year and five months old. As he was still very young and Kristine was a very calm child, we doubled the attention we gave to the boy.

When Kilden was two, things started to happen. At the beginning I didn't take much notice of them, but then Kilden would become agitated and angry, saying that he was Alexandre and not Kilden.

'You silly! I'm not Kilden. I am Alexandre!'

This was quite normal, because his names were Kilden Alexandre. It didn't matter if he preferred his second one.

On other occasions he would exclaim:

'I'm not Kilden, you silly! I am the priest! I am Alexandre!'

'Oh! So you want to be a priest?', we would say.

'No! I'm not going to be a priest! I am the priest!'

It didn't mean anything to me at the time. It was just his opinion, and I had other things on my mind. Kilden's outbursts only meant that he was a temperamental child and could be aggressive even with his mother, because several times he had called me bad words, that no one at home used, when trying to explain that he was the "priest".

Although I was no longer a Roman Catholic, going to

masses, communion and processions, I had not accepted any other religion. I had never studied Spiritism, nor did I accept their ideas as being the truth, and I thought I knew enough to know what others knew, rightly or wrongly – that Spiritism is a diabolical sect for the ignorant, whom it turns mad. That was more or less what I thought.

But there was one detail: in my opinion, the Roman Catholic religion was not very Christian. So, I felt I was a Christian but not a Roman Catholic. It was a regrettable for me and for those who knew me at school that I was no longer a practising Catholic. It never occurred to me that the words of my son Kilden Alexandre might have a spiritual meaning, or anything to do with reincarnation.

But then, one afternoon two strange things happened. I asked Kildary to go to the shop and buy something, I can't remember what. While he was out I took Kilden to have a bath.

It was early in 1983. A promising year for me, as I was thinking of writing something that had to do with spiritual and artistic themes. After a few days of retrospection I had written 'A Symphony of Prayers'. But let's go back to Kilden's bath.

I wrapped him up in a towel and took him to the bedroom in order to get him dressed. On my way to the room I asked him:

'Where did Mummy find this little sweetie? Eh?'

I always used to joke with the children like this. They always answered that I had fetched them from the hospital. Keila, however, used to say: 'it was in the Count's house...'

Kilden's answer puzzled me. With wide-open eyes and speaking seriously, the boy said:

'You know! I was on a motorcycle. Then a truck came and hit the motorcycle. It fell over, and I hit my head on the ground, and I died, and went down there…and then you got another me!'

Startled by that answer, I asked him:

'When did this happen?'

'When I was a priest! My motorcycle fell over and I went down into the hole... and you got another me.'

'What about the truck?

'It went a long way away.'

I left him on the bed, half dressed, and went to the other room to write down what he had said. That answer would give any disbeliever something to think about. It had to be recorded.

I remembered Kilden's yells when he was called by his first name. I remembered that he was always saying he was the priest. I also recalled June 1st, 1972 when Radio Guarani announced the death of Father Jonathan, my best friend, in an accident on Amazonina Avenue. My God, my head was going round in circles!

I sat down in the living room in a daze. It was only then that I noticed that Kildary had not returned from the shop. I saw him covered with mud, hands bleeding, and his face bruised. I thought he might have fallen and hurt himself: the images alternated in my mind - little Kilden telling his story, Father Jonathan having a road accident and Kildary hurt.

Imagine my shock when Kildary came in, dirty and bruised, just as I had foreseen a few minutes before.

Impressed with myself as I was, I didn't even ask what had happened. I took his jacket off and put some medicine on his scratches, which fortunately were not deep. Kildary had climbed up a small mound and had fallen down it.

A few days later, I went to see Mr Jota Bueno, a Spiritist friend of my husband. He was not at home but at a meeting in Mr J. S. Pereira's house. Mr Pereira had been the leader of the Family Christian Movement, arranging meetings between couples in the Diocese, courses for those who were engaged and so on. He was a good friend of the Bishop and always travelled with him.

Once, Mr Pereira had felt ill and the doctors could not help him, so he decided to go to a meeting at the Spiritist Centre and he was cured. After much thought, Mr. Pereira sought the Bishop, his friend Dom Claudio, and told him that from then on he would become a practicing Spiritist, just as he had been a Catholic before. But he didn't want to lose Dom Claudio's friendship.

Mr Bueno and Mr Pereira were chatting about Spiritism when I got there. I sat down with them, in a large and comfortable room. They were talking about religious syncretism in the state of Bahia.

I told them about my problem, since they were friends.

Mr Bueno listened to my story and showed no surprise. He had been a Spiritist for a long time. Mr Pereira, however, was astonished.

'Watch your boy from now on,' said Mr Bueno. 'You'll

see that he has much in common with the "dead" Father Jonathan. Perhaps he has come to do what he could not do for you when he was incarnated as a priest. It's certain that he will not be a priest in this incarnation. It's up to you to guide him along the right way. Something remained to be done in the past, and now as mother and son you have something to accomplish... It's not surprising. Everything is natural. Reincarnation is very natural. Don't be frightened, because you will learn how things are in due course. Keep your eyes open and always do your best to help.

'As for the noises,' he went on, 'they are spirits who have been assigned to show you that there is a spiritual world, and to prepare you for a new revelation, which is the reincarnation of your friend the priest as your son Kilden. It could also be that Father Jonathan's friends have not left him definitively, and are making noises in your house after the birth of your son.

'What happened, my dear Marine, is that God, through the spirits, wants to make you conscious of a mission you have been seeking for a long time and still have not found. It's up to you to find your way from now on.'

I left Mr Pereira's house feeling relieved and encouraged. Yet suddenly I was filled with doubt: What if he had returned for revenge? What if my affection had stirred up some inappropriate thoughts, or if my marriage had made him angry? Father Jonathan, now as Kilden, might cause discord in my life. Oh Lord!

The following week I started going to meetings at the Spiritist centre. I felt at ease there. They had a good library and I started reading eagerly, more out of curiosity than to get closer to the spiritual life. I have always wanted to learn, to question, and to be aware of what I am doing. I was not made for half measures. That was why I had to delve deeply. The few people who could answer my questions never satisfied me entirely, and I was always reading, listening and feeling things from another world. I watched Mr. Pereira's wife, with a pencil and paper, week after week, trying to get a spiritual message through automatic writing, but nothing happened.

Once Mr Bueno asked me:

'Did you feel anything, Marine?'

'No, nothing!'

'Look. I saw a scene around you. It seemed like a moonlight night. In Vienna... but I can't give and other details... It wasn't clear...'

However, before all these things with Kilden Alexandre and everything I described above happened, we were in B.H. on one occasion, at midday, in our car. The radio was on and we were going into the city centre. My husband was talking to his nephew Saulo, who was driving the car for us.

The radio played some music that transported me away from that busy part of the city. I felt I was in a familiar place. The moonlight reflected on the leaves... Along a beautiful avenue... Lovely horses, hunting dogs, and me...

The moonlight enchanted me. I heard the music on the radio as if it was coming out of the forest, on which the moonlight was shining... Someone, not quite in focus but very white, frightened me... I tortured myself trying to make those images clearer.

The music stopped. I became aware of the city with its cars, people and busy commerce, and Marcinho talking to Saulo.

A few years later there was a record fair in the main square of Oliva. As Marcinho could not go, he asked a friend to choose and buy two records of his choice for us, which he did. One of them was "Vienna's Greatest Waltzes", and when I heard one of the tracks I was startled to find myself having the same feeling I had had in the city. It was the same tune I had heard on the car radio: Tales from the Vienna Woods.

As time went by, I noticed that the anxiety attacks that Kilden had when he was asleep coincided with my prayers that Alexandre's soul should appear to me. When I became aware of this, I stopped invoking him.

One afternoon I was with the children packing the suitcases for the trip we were going to make. While taking some papers out of a large trunk, a black and white postcard fell to the floor. It was so well hidden that I had forgotten all about it. Kildary and Kilden picked it up. Sitting on the floor Kilden then said:

'Look! This is where I lived and that's where Mummy lived down there.' Kilden put his finger on the Priests' School (which I used to call the "building on the hill") and on the Nuns' School where I was a boarder.

Feeling curious, I asked him what he used to do in that big house.

'I played soccer with all the boys, you silly! You ought to know!'

'When did you play soccer with the boys?' I asked him.

'When I was a priest!' Kilden yelled impatiently.

Kildary looked at me, laughing, not knowing why I was so surprised.

Kilden Alexandre, kneeling and sitting on his heels, lowered his head and continued looking at the postcard as if we weren't there. Sometimes the boy isolated himself in meditation, sucking his comforter and with the corner of the pillow on his nose. Although he could be naughty, he had moments like this.

Surprised, I picked up the photo and read what was written in Father Jonathan's handwriting on the back:

"Marine, what a lot of unforgettable memories this photo brings back! Memories that will remain alive forever for you and for Alexandre."

The pain caused by Father Jonathan's absence got mixed up with the nightmare caused by such a tiny little boy who insisted that he was Alexandre, the priest.

On another occasion, Marcinho bought a record by the singer Paulo Sérgio. On listening to the first song, "Última Canção" (Last Song) I noticed that Kilden, who was lying on the sofa with his head buried in his arms, was crying.

'What's the matter? Why are you crying?' I asked him.

'The music makes me sad,' he said.

'Why, if you don't even know the music?'

'Yes, I do. I'm Alexandre!', he exclaimed.

This is why, after a lot of suffering , reading, and trying to find out what was going on, I decided to ask the priests at the

Lyceum in B. H., where Father Jonathan spent his last year, for a biography of the person who somehow disrupted a period of my youth, and now returned to disturb or improve my path in life.

Here follows part of the material I eventually received from the Lyceum priests:

FATHER JONATHAN (1924 – 1972)

"What marked Father Jonathan's life was his selfless dedication to helping others. He never slowed down, yet he never seemed tired. I can truly say that Father Jonathan shaped a community. If today it is an efficient and active one, this is thanks to Father Jonathan's ten years of work.

From 1958 to 1968 his work and unlimited dedication turned around a district with 15.000 inhabitants. Needless to say, his concern was always for the young. We remember the many soccer teams that he formed, encouraged and directed. He was the priest of the humble man. Always smiling, he solved the most intricate problems with the gentle manner people from this State. At times he was uncompromising, especially when speaking of certain fashions which he considered improper and would not condone.

He showed no fear when things went wrong. He was firm and said what had to be said, shaming the man or the woman involved. I lived nine years with Father Jonathan. It may seem strange, but we never disagreed or quarrelled. His was a life of work, sacrifice, and dedication. He was humble and obedient. He never needed or asked for anything, never complained about the food, living quarters or clothes. He was extraordinary in this respect.

He was slandered but never complained openly, keeping to himself some people's lack of understanding. He was incapable of getting angry, seeking revenge, or speaking ill of anyone. I never heard him saying an impolite word.

At his funeral, he was praised publicly by State Congressman P.F., who described his role in the building of a new church and sports centre – 'All thanks to the untiring effort of Father Jonathan, who dedicated all his life to the Community of the Poor. His greatest wish was to improve their social condition.'

Father Jonathan must have been in a deep coma when I heard him calling me in my kitchen that evening in 1972, and dreamed of him stretching out his hands, trying to pull me over to a better place, where the lilies scented the air.

PART THREE

The years went by.

In 1985 Marcinho realised his old dream. He sold everything he had acquired in the city of Oliva and we went to live in the city of J. S., which he had always liked. Our daughter Kléria was born there in 1986.

Although we came to J. S. in a good financial condition, we got into trouble very soon. It was a hard time for us. But our losses were only material ones, since we gained in the spiritual area. We matured, came to a better understanding of things, and we were able to teach our children the true values of life. In Oliva, life had been too comfortable and selfish.

Since he was very young, Kilden Alexandre had been more restless than the others, but as time went by, two things have happened.

1 - Kilden no longer claims to be Alexandre the priest, and can not remember what he had said before on the subject.

2 - Kilden and Marcinho do not get on with each other. Ever since Kilden was very small, his father would spank him in fits of rage in which he said he could kill him. Admittedly, Marcinho does try hard to make peace with Kilden, taking him for walks at weekends, chatting with him and giving him advice. Kilden promises to be good during the week. But suddenly everything changes. If he makes a minor mistake when reading, or quarrels with his sisters, Marcinho gets his belt and beats him hard, pulls his ears or punches his head.

It hurts me to see my child suffering and there are times

when everything ends in total misunderstanding between Marcinho, Kilden and me.

There is something else I don't understand: if the child is really Father Jonathan, why is he so slow in learning to read? Father Jonathan taught thousands of people to read and write.

Kilden adores playing soccer and, as his father says, he is good with a ball, as Jonathan also was. He had formed several teams and was always playing soccer with the boys.

Father Jonathan made friends easily with blacks, whites, poor, rich, men, women and children. So does Kilden. He gets involved easily with people, and every time we go out we meet someone he recognises..

We are always together. On Sundays, he is the first one to get up and go to Catechism and Mass. (Everybody at home goes to Mass except me). In spite of this, he also goes to the Spiritist Centre with me.

Kilden says he is going to be a pilot when he grows up. He likes dangerous things, which worries me. Unlike Kildary, who is quieter, Kilden never stops. And speaking of Kildary, he is now doing the 1st year of Philosophy at the seminary. He is very responsible and studious. He still says he wants to be a priest, but Kilden has shown no such inclination so far.

* * *

That is the end of Marine Waterloo's report. We will now analyse this case from the parapsychological point of view, in order to assess the value of its contents as evidence for the reincarnation hypothesis.

Although we found numerous facts that suggest that Kilden is Father Jonathan reborn, we must examine hypotheses other that of reincarnation that could explain it.

* * *

CHAPTER II

ANALYSIS OF THE EVIDENCE

"However, if ostensible memories of past lives are not considered satisfactory proof of reincarnation, what other type of evidence could there be to uphold this doctrine?"

Ken Wilber *("Morte, Renascimento e Meditação", in* **"Explorações Contemporâneas da Vida Depois da Morte**, *São Paulo, Cultrix, 1992, p. 164.)*

RELEVANT FACTS THAT PRECEDED THE BIRTH OF KILDEN ALEXANDRE

A careful examination of the above report reveals that there a number of important passages which suggest the manifestation of paranormal phenomena that occurred before the birth of Dona Marine's fourth child. This suggests that the connection established in life between Dona Marine and Father Jonathan remained intact even after the latter's death.

In the large bibliography of paranormal phenomena compiled by the researchers of the Society for Psychical Research (SPR) established in London in 1882, there is a section devoted to the numerous cases collected by three of its founder-members and published in the book *Phantasms of the Living* by Edmund Gurney, Frederic W. H. Myers and Frank Podmore,

It deals with paranormal communications occurring

between people who are still alive. The most common of these occur in circumstances of crisis, especially at the time of death. They are the so-called **Warnings of Death**, and the book contains about one thousand well documented cases of people who appeared visibly, or gave other types of signs to friends or relatives they cared for, informing them of their death. Usually, these messages coincide with the comatose state of the communicator who is about to die, but is still alive. This explains the reason for the title: *Phantasms of the Living*. The most dramatic are those who produce intelligible signs; for example: they appear visibly, speak and give their warnings verbally, make noises, move objects or speak, while remaining invisible, calling people by their names or giving advice, influencing people during their sleep, showing themselves and saying they have just died, causing symbolic dreams that can be interpreted correctly, and so on.

Others limit themselves to causing strong intuitions or premonitions, induced telepathically. Some manage to influence pets, even at long distance.

In the case of Dona Marine Waterloo, Father Jonathan warned her of his death three times.

1) First Warning: The Priest's Voice.

Dona Marine was awake. Here is her account in full:

"Let us return to my kitchen on the night of May 31st, 1972. I was near the stove, preparing a feeding bottle for the baby, before Kildary woke up and started crying."

"The house was closed. Marcinho was in his shop talking with friends. It was usual for friends living in S. N. to meet in shops when they close. In our house there were only Kildary, asleep, and me, awake."

"A black and white plastic curtain made of strings hung from the door that separated the kitchen from the sitting room. My back was turned to the curtain while I was preparing the feeding bottle, when I heard Father Jonathan's voice calling my name. I turned round quickly and saw the curtain moving as if someone had passed through it.

"Frightened, I turned the stove off and ran to the bedroom. I lay down and started to analyse the occurrence: Why did I turn to attend to Father Jonathan when I hadn't seen him since 1969? Where was he now? Why did we separate? Why did we stay apart?

"The last time I heard from him was in July 1970, when he wrote to tell me about his apostleship in B.H. Why hadn't I written to him?

"I concluded that marriage is solitude for two, and that the priest might not have called me after all. I was not quite right in the head after Kildary's birth."

"When Marcinho arrived, I told him what had happened and he said it might be mental tiredness."

"I went to sleep."

Could it be that D. Marine was a victim of a simple subjective illusion due to supposed mental fatigue?

It was not so late at night when she was preparing the baby's bottle. She was waiting for her husband to arrive and, it seems that she was still wide awake. Besides, who or what moved the strings of the curtain as if someone had passed through it?

There was no draught at that moment.

Another strange fact is the coincidence between the two simultaneous events, which occurred on this occasion: the voice that called her that she identified as being that of Father Jonathan, and the abnormal movement of the curtain. It seems this was not simply a subjective illusion caused by exhausted nerves or tiredness.

2) Second Warning: The Dream.

After the voice of the priest, together with the movement of the strings of the curtain, another phenomenon happened which had all the features of a **Warning of Death**. Here is the description from D. Marine's Report:

"I slept and dreamed that a huge plantation of lilies separated myself from Father Jonathan who, from the other side, stretched his hands toward me. His arms, immensely long, tried to touch me. My hands also tried to touch his but couldn't. When I took a few steps trying to get to the other side, my feet sank in the mud. The enormous bed of lilies was on a swamp. Father Jonathan said: "Come, it's better on this side! Come with me, Marine! Everything out there is so sad..." And his arms grew tremendously in an effort to pull me, but to no avail and I woke up."

It is interesting to note that D. Marine had no premonition, no intuition that she was being warned of Father Jonathan's imminent death. Only memories of her boarding school came to mind.

3) Third Warning: Communication of Father Jonathan's Death.

Let us note that Father Jonathan gave a third and final

warning, though he must have been clinically dead at the time.

G. N. M. Tyrrell, in his book **Apparitions**, criticised the interpretation given to certain kinds of apparitions mentioned in **Phantasms of the Living**, by Edmund Gurney, one of its authors. He relates most of these manifestations to **simple coincidences**. For this reason, Gurney classifies them as mere subjective hallucinations, created by the individual's imagination.

Tyrrell contests Gurney's point of view, showing that most of the cases are authentic manifestations implying communication between people. Tyrrell also admits the possibility of a tangible communication between the dead and the living, not only at the moment of death, but in other circumstances. (Tyrrell, 1973, pp. 32 e 33)

He divides apparitions into four main groups:

I. Communications obtained during experiments in which one person deliberately tries to show himself visibly to another person or communicate with them by any means, but not in critical situations.

II. Apparitions, sensations of touch, voices, etc. of a distant person who is undergoing a major crisis.

III. Apparitions, voices, noises, touches or other kinds of sensation that enable the author to be recognised as soon as death occurs, but without the warned person's previous knowledge of any such crisis related to the dead person. Whoever sees, hears or perceives an apparition may not have had any previous information regarding the one that is manifesting.

IV. Spirits or apparitions that usually haunt houses or places. (Tyrrell, 1975, p.33)

In this case, D. Marine had experiences that fit perfectly in the second and third of Tyrrell's groups. Father Jonathan's last manifestation was as follows, according to the Report:

"Next day, June 1st 1972, was a holy day, dedicated to "Corpus Christi". Marcinho was going to close his shop so that we could follow the procession. Kildary and I were ready, waiting for him. I went to the shop to tell my husband it was time to close it. When I was returning to the house, Marcinho called me by name. I turned around. However, the voice I heard was Father Jonathan's and not Marcinho's.

"I went in. But I had hardly closed the door when Marcinho, who was listening to Radio Guarani, went out to the street and called me. I went back to the shop.

'What was the name of that friend of yours, the priest?', he asked me, turning off the radio.

'Father Jonathan.', I said.

'He has just died in a hospital, in B.H. He had a car accident in Amazonina Avenue. He had a relapse yesterday and died today.'

This last episode completes and makes sense of the first two incidents. It is obviously Father Jonathan's classic **Warning of Death.** He tried to tell D. Marine that he was on the point of death.

Modern parapsychology now includes the study of Near-Death Experiences (NDE). Such cases, at first considered to be simple hallucinations caused by cerebral disturbances, due to lack of oxygen and other correlated factors, have been widely and scientifically investigated by numerous doctors and psychologists. We know from thousands of statements made by people who were clinically dead and were resuscitated, that even during the period when there was an absence of signs of life, most of them were conscious. They also felt they left their bodies and were able to see their surroundings, even seeing their own lifeless bodies. Some of them saw the dramatic effort doctors and nurses made while trying to bring them back to life. Others felt they were sliding through a tunnel, at the end of which they saw a "Being of Light" waiting for them and who greeted them most warmly. The experiences are varied but they follow the same pattern. (Moody, Jr., 1975, 1977, 1988, 1992; Ritchie, 1980; Sabom, 1982; Morse and Perry, 1990; Ring, 1992; Mercier, 1992)

It seems that, in general, at the moment of leaving the body due to death, spirits can feel sufficiently lucid and free to seek those they love most. In some of these cases the phenomenon of **Warning of Death** may occur. It is likely that something similar took place between Father Jonathan and D. Marine.

Could it be that D. Marine did not often dream of Father Jonathan, because of the affection she felt for him, aggravated by his absence? In her Report she mentions that she did have difficulties dreaming about him in spite of her intense desire to see him, even if only in dreams. The situation remained unchanged after his death:

"I went on praying for Father Jonathan to appear. But I only dreamt of him twice, unimportant dreams which I have forgotten."

Therefore, there is good evidence that Father Jonathan felt strongly attached to D. Marine, and his spirit probably sought her when he was getting detached from his body. This instance of **Warning of Death** allows one to form the

hypothesis that Father Jonathan's spirit had been in touch with D. Marine during the 7 years, 2 months and 24 days which elapsed before the moment of Kilden's conception, when his definitive reincarnatory connection took place. Unfortunately there are no ways of investigating more directly what happens during this very short intermission period, in order to know exactly what happens between death and the beginning of the next incarnation.

However, the short intermission period in this case is one more item of evidence in favour of the reincarnation hypothesis. Statistical findings show that children able to remember previous incarnations generally go through an intermission period that is very short. The median intermission time counted by the earthly calendar for such children is approximately six years, but can vary from 0 to 32 years.

Nowadays, for normal people who do not remember past lives, the intermission time is approximately 250 years. (Goldstein, 1991)

The short period of time between Father Jonathan's death and his alleged reincarnation as Kilden, is close to the world average as shown above. This favours the reincarnation hypothesis.

The short intermission time also explains why children such as Kilden recall episodes connected with their previous lives, especially those which were marked by dramatic events and/or intense suffering by the prior personality. Moments of great happiness can also leave memories of this kind.

STRANGE PHENOMENA ENCOUNTERED AFTER KILDEN ALEXANDRE'S BIRTH

'After Kilden's birth, there was an inexplicable change in our home,' D. Marine stated in her report. An antagonism or rejection of the father toward the child that was to be born showed itself during pregnancy.

'Marcinho got upset with my pregnancy,' she said when talking about the episode of her trying to get a job at a new agency which was to be opened in their home town.

She got the first place in a contest but could not take the job because the agency had been inaugurated during the month of May 1980, when Kilden was born. As D. Marine could not take the job, she lost it in favour of the next applicant.

Was this the only reason for the dislike shown towards the child that was about to be born? Wouldn't there be an old rivalry between the two spirits who disliked each other, and whose past demanded the reconciliation necessary for their evolution? Life has a way of creating such dramas, which are planned and acted out by the people themselves with the aim oftheir perfection.

According to D. Marine's Report, "Kilden was a good child and slept well." However "during his sleep, his breathing became fast and he gasped, making quite a lot of noise." D. Marine thought: "He is dreaming," and would change his position.

What would a new-born baby dream about to make it show signs of distress? Would it be because of some organic trouble? D. Marine doesn't clear up this point and gives no further information. It seems that the symptoms were not alarming.

However, strange things did occur. This is how D. Marine describes them:

"One night at 9 pm. I was sitting on my bed feeding the baby. There was a small nightstand between the bed and the wall. The kids were already asleep in the next room. Everything was quiet and I was looking at Kilden's face while he sucked, keeping his eyes closed.

"I suddenly heard several knocks coming from the small nightstand, about one foot away from me. Frightened, I lay down on the bed and started to call Kildary; the poor boy came running. I asked him if he had heard anything and he said he heard loud knocks in my room. Trembling, I put the baby on the bed and stood up. My legs were shaking, so I asked Kildary if he would go to the kitchen and get me a glass of water.

"When Kildary was about to leave the room we heard steps of many people running from the kitchen. A loud noise, as if these people had knocked against the refrigerator with their hands. The refrigerator was right opposite our bedroom door. Kildary screamed, moved away, and fell down on a chair. The noise continued, came in the direction of my room, and then turned towards the bathroom, where it ceased.

"I felt as if several people were holding on to each other, as if they were playing at being a train. The noise was of the steps of several people running and jumping."

D. Marine ended her report of these facts saying that neither she nor Kildary wanted to talk about what happened. She then described countless inexplicable phenomena that took place later on, strange and varied noises which occurred for no obvious reason:

"One night at midnight, Marcinho and I were in the kitchen having a cup of coffee and chatting. During weekends he got in late from work. It was Saturday. The house was clean and silent. The kids were asleep. Suddenly we heard loud knocks in the pantry near the kitchen.

"In the pantry there was an icebox, a table with the chairs, a small cupboard and a special pen for the baby.

"The moment I heard the noise I jumped up and ran over to Marcinho. The noise could be heard again, stronger and clearer. Marcinho also heard it. The first time, the noise seemed to come from near the cupboard. Doubtless, the second time it came from the baby's pen. We went to the pantry. Nothing. Everything was quiet and undisturbed.

"On another night, at 9:00 pm, we were already in bed. Only Marcinho was working. I heard the noise of high heels outside the window of my room. There was a ramp toward the porch right below the window of my room.

"I raised my head and waited for someone to call or knock at the door.

"No one called. No one knocked. The high heel steps continued inside my room, from the dressing table to Kilden's cot. Full of fear, I covered my head and called Kildary, who came quickly. Again I put them all in my bed and locked the door, waiting for Marcinho to arrive.

"A few days later, again at 9 pm, I was lying down and Kilden was asleep, when suddenly I saw a figure near the cot - a figure that disappeared soon afterwards.

"Once, we went to bed much earlier than usual and as I was tired, I soon fell asleep. I woke up hearing the noise of Marcinho's car coming down our street and entering the garage. My husband then banged the door of the car, closed the gate and went up toward the porch, with his keys rattling. As usual, I heard then the noise of the key in the lock of the door. I also heard Marcinho tap the door with the key, because the other key had remained in the lock inside the room. I got up fast and opened the door, meaning to tell my husband that I was so sleepy that I forgot to take the key out. Then I saw that the porch was empty, the door of the garage was open and that neither our car nor Marcinho were there. Frightened, I ran inside and closed the door. I looked at the watch. It was 9:10 pm

"I took the key out of the lock and went to my room, unable to understand what was happening."

D. Marine said her house was being rebuilt, to make it larger and more comfortable. But those noises continued to bother her. She felt discouraged. Although D. Marine doesn't consider herself to be paranormal, there are numerous facts that indicate that she is. In fact, D. Marine makes this clear not only because of the recent happenings, which we have already examined, but also due to others that happened when she was quite young:

"The noises that I heard during my sleepless nights during my childhood were understood by my parents to be due to fear. Things that happen to children who can't get to sleep. Just imagination.

"But now? I was no longer a child. The noises continued. My sons heard them. Once my husband also heard them. My house is not haunted. Noises occur wherever I am. I'm not paranormal, but I feel something strange in me. I'm afraid I'm going crazy."

Because of our experience and out of the respect due to D. Marine, we dare affirm that she does have paranormal gifts, especially of **psychokinesis**. The phenomena she described and we transcribed point to certain typical cases of **poltergeist** activity, but are rather mild compared to those we have recorded. In technical terms, D. Marine acts as an **epicentre** – the person who makes the production of phenomena possible, in spite of the fact that their participation is unconscious and, "ipso facto", involuntary.

Yet it remains to be seen what are the agents who produce the noises. We might say that in accordance with our experience some noises, but perhaps not all of them, were produced by the spirit of Father Jonathan. This might sound foolish, but we will try to give a plausible explanation.

The reincarnation process seems to start soon after the two gametes merge in the fecundation process after which the **zygote** is formed. **Once the Biological Organing Model (BOM)** of the spirit is linked to the ovum, the operation continues gradually as far as the successive mitosis duplication of the embryo cells occurs. During the period in which the foetus is formed, the BOM will gain more territory in the incipient being, guiding the disposition of the cells of the newly growing organism.

The connection proceeds, step by step, but there is always a larger portion of the spirit which is outside the body in the process of formation. This free part of the spirit remains out of our space even after birth and during our whole life. One can say that in the new-born baby the spirit is almost entirely outside the child's body. It can thus be said that the baby has two personalities:

One is developing under the guidance of the BOM. The personality in formation is still semi-unconscious, with the normal instincts and reflexes prevailing. It will change later under the morphogenetic influence of the BOM and biological heredity combined with adaptation to the influence of the environment in which the child will develop.

In the first stages of growth the personality is like clay in the potter's hands. It brings the essential qualities of the generic characters inherited from the parents, plus the spirit's potentialities acquired in past lives. These last ones are a kind of spiritual self-inheritance which Buddhists call Sankharâ (Andrade 1984, pp. 203-205). So it is possible to educate the person during infancy, thus building a new personality. It will naturally suffer the influence of the previous personality's character, including its phobias, tastes, mannerisms and so on, but to a lesser degree. It can thus improve itself and its qualities by acquiring new knowledge and experience. The parents, teachers and friends, as well as the restrictions and aggressions of the new life, represent the work of the potter.

Let us now see what happens to the other part of the spirit, which is located outside the baby's body. This part is made up of what was left over from the previous personality, that is: a vital body, an astral body, and resulting from these two bodies, a spiritual body in process of disappearance in order to give place eventually to the new physical body in development.

With respect to the phenomenon mentioned before, which happens at birth, we quote from the **Encyclopaedia of Psychic Science**:

"On the basis of some curious experiments in regression

of memory, Colonel Rochas believes that the double is only complete at seven years of age, and that the astral shape enters the body a little while before birth and then only partially. Maxwell studied a very sensitive young woman who was entrusted with the bringing up of a child from her birth. She saw at its side a luminous shadow with features more formed that those of the child, and rather larger than it. This shadow, at its birth, was further away from the child. It seemed to penetrate gradually into the body. At fourteen months of age the penetration was about two-thirds complete." (Fodor, 1974, p. 100).

When the individual is still in gestation, and later as newly born, that part of the Spirit, not yet integrated in the body of the newly born, can in some cases can be owned by a portion of the conscience of the previous personality. In this situation, the previous personality sometimes gets to act as a free spirit. Finding an "epicentre" at its disposal, it can cause **physical phenomena** such as noises, footsteps and imitations of other sounds.

We think that Father Jonathan's spirit was trying to give signs of his presence in this way. It is necessary to take into consideration that, in the reincarnation phase, the previous personality located in the free part of the spirit, may not have the ownership of its full conscience. For this reason, in this case its acts would be less rational, more confused and strange, being equal to a highly disturbed or intoxicated person's behaviour.

These are the reasons why we suppose there were attempts to communicate on the part of the residue of Father Jonathan's personality on that occasion. It is also possible that other spiritual entities took advantage of the occasion to produce a small "poltergeist". There are many spirits who are not evolved that enjoy frightening people.

However, we have to remember that we are only making conjectures about situations still dependent on demonstrating a stronger premise, that is, that Kilden is really the reincarnation of Father Jonathan. The objective of this work is to verify the validity of the first hypothesis. We are not, therefore, definitely affirming either of these suppositions. Our verdict will be reached at the end of this book.

Finally, we should explain that in poltergeist cases that we have investigated, we came across one case in which the phenomena happening matched with the time of pregnancy of the "epicentre" – a married woman. (Andrade, 1988b, Cap. III)

In poltergeist cases, the presence of an epicentre is practically essential. Paranormal phenomena of a physical nature may occur exceptionally in the absence of a human agent, but such a fact is not always of the poltergeist type. It is usually a case of haunting. In D. Marine's case one can suspect two persons who could have acted as epicentre: the first son, Kildary, then 8 years old, and D. Marine herself.

It is unlikely that young Kildary should have been the epicentre. It is more likely that D. Marine was the agent. In a long questionnaire, which we put to her, there was one question about the paranormal manifestations that occurred with her. From her answer we learned that D. Marine experienced many phenomena of this kind, which always happened in her presence. Therefore, she probably was the epicentre of incidents that happened when Kildary was still a baby.

Once Father Jonathan's reincarnation as Kilden is demonstrated, the paranormal phenomena will be a highly significant factor in the elaboration of a hypothesis that explains the process of rebirth.

Let us now analyse the subject's first memories.

FIRST MEMORIES

1) Started to say he was not Kilden but Alexandre when he was 2 years old.

From D. Marine Waterloo's report:

"When Kilden was two years old, things started to happen. At the beginning I didn't pay too much attention. Kilden became nervous and angry saying that he was Alexandre and not Kilden.

"You silly! I'm not Kilden. I am Alexandre!

"That was not really important, because his name was Kilden Alexandre. It was not important if he preferred his second name."

In fact, for someone like D. Marine, who had a strictly Catholic education, it would be very unlikely that the supposition that her son was Father Jonathan's reincarnation would occur to her. Besides, let us consider the special circumstance of the boy having a double name, Kilden Alexandre. It would be very natural that, although only two years old, he showed preference for the second name, Alexandre.

This aversion to the idea of the possibility of reincarnation on the part of D. Marine is shown more clearly in the following episode:

2) Sometimes, perhaps upset because he was not understood, Kilden cried angrily that he was the Priest!

"On other occasions he would cry:

'I'm not Kilden, you silly! I am the priest! I am Alexandre!'

"Oh! So you're going to be a priest", we would say.

'No! I'm not going to be a priest! I am the Priest!'

"It meant nothing to me. It was only the boy's point of view.

Kilden's outbursts only showed that he was a temperamental child and was aggressive even with his mother, because several times he had called her bad words that no one in the family used, when trying to explain that he was the priest.

At that time D.Marine, a mature and somewhat disillusioned woman, was "no longer a Roman Catholic, going to masses, communion and processions" as she put it in her report, when she discussed this incident from Kilden's childhood.

However, she had still not considered the idea of adopting any other sect or religious philosophy, much less Spiritism. She held the general view, especially that of Catholics, that "Spiritism is the work of the devil, it is only for the ignorant and drives those who get involved in it mad."

In her report, D Marine insisted that "It never occurred to me that the words of my son Kilden Alexandre might have a spiritual meaning or anything to do with reincarnation. In his outbursts he made it quite clear that he was not "going to be" a priest. He "was" the priest."

D. Marine told us personally that the wife of her husband's brother and her two daughters lived at that time, in the same town of Oliva. They witnessed several times events described above, such as "Kilden crying out that he was the priest, that he wasn't Kilden and that he was Alexandre".

However, not even her relatives guessed that Kilden was speaking about his past life identification as a priest. In those days, in the interior of the state of Minas Gerais the predominant religion was Roman Catholicism. Very few people knew what reincarnation was.

Even nowadays, such ideas are considered as being "Spiritist matters", and people believe that those who get involved with Spiritism end up by going mad. The Devil would possess the souls of these imprudent people, etc, etc... These ideas were massively disseminated through sermons and pseudo-scientific literature, guided by the Catholic clergy. So it is hardly surprising that not only Dona Marine but also her relatives, all traditional Catholics, took no notice of Kilden's claims that **he was the priest**.

Father Jonathan had agreed with the pseudonym Alexandre that D. Marine had given him during his lifetime. But a very young child would not have the name Jonathan stored in his immature brain, so for this reason the priest used his pseudonym, which was also one of the child's names - Alexandre.

However, he managed to overcome his identification difficulty, as follows:

3) After a bath, Kilden was able to make his mother understand that he was the reincarnation of the priest.

D. Marine had asked her elder son Kildary to go to a store in order to buy something (she does not remember what). Then she took Kilden to the bathroom. The child was less than three years old.

After his bath, she wrapped him in a towel and took him to the bedroom to get him dressed. As she says:

"On my way to the room I asked him:

'Where did Mummy find this dear little fellow?'

"I always joked with the children like this. They always answered that it was in the hospital. Keila, however, used to say: "it was in the Count's house..."

"Kilden's answer puzzled me. With wide-open eyes and speaking seriously, the boy said:

'You know! I was on my motorcycle. Then a truck come and hit the motorcycle. I fell down, hit my head and died. I went down deep and then you got another me'.

"Frightened by that answer, I asked him:

'When, did this happen?'

'When I was a priest! My motorcycle stayed on the ground and I went down deep in the hole... and you got another me!'

'And the truck?'

'The truck went away...'

"I left him on the bed, half dressed, and went to the other room to write down what he had said. That answer would disturb any non-believer. It had to be recorded.

"I remembered Kilden's protests when he was called by his first name. I remembered that he was always saying he was the priest. I also remembered June 1st, 1972 when Radio Guarani announced the death of Father Jonathan, my best friend... An accident on Amazonina Avenue. My God, my head was spinning! ..."

With this episode D. Marine finally had a revelation regarding the origin of Kilden's reactions when they called him by his first name. But even so she had trouble in accepting the evidence she herself had seen. It was too much for a person born, bred and educated in a religious environment which taught exactly the opposite.

Only much later, after consulting Spiritist leaders and having read books on Spiritism, did D. Marine get used to the idea of reincarnation, accepting it as the best explanation for Kilden's behaviour.

4) Spontaneous recognition of a photograph of some places where, as Father Jonathan, he had met D. Marine at her College.

"One afternoon I was in a room with the children packing the suitcases for the trip we were going to make.

"While taking some papers out of a large trunk a black and white postcard fell down. It was so well hidden that I had forgotten all about it. Kildary and Kilden picked it up. Sitting on the floor Kilden then said:

'Look! This is were I lived and Mummy lived down there.'

"The photo was of the school in N. P., where I studied and where I got to know Father Jonathan in 1968."

5) Kilden recalled the time when he was a priest and played soccer with the children, becoming impatient when his mother gave the impression of ignoring this detail.

At the time when the photograph in question was picked up by Kildary and his brother Kilden, the latter seems to have recalled more details regarding his previous incarnation. Intrigued, D. Marine observed his behaviour.

At one point, Kilden put his little finger on the Priests' College and then on the Sisters' College, where D. Marine had been a boarder. Those images probably awakened, by association of ideas, certain memories in Kilden. D. Marine, who was watching him attentively, tried to test him by asking him what he was doing in that "big house", referring to the priest's college, where the male students lived. Kilden immediately answered:

"I played soccer with the boys, you silly! You ought to know!"

D. Marine decided to confirm if he was really remembering his past life and insisted:

"When did you play soccer with the boys? I asked him.

"When I was a priest!' Kilden cried impatiently."

It seems obvious that the related picture should have provoked some reaction in Kilden, if we admit, if only as a working hypothesis, that he is Father Jonathan reborn. This is how D. Marine described what happened when Kilden saw the photograph:

"Kildary (the oldest son) looked at me laughing, not understanding why I was so surprised.

"Kilden Alexandre, kneeling and sitting on his heels, lowered his head and continued to look at the postcard as if we weren't there. Sometimes the boy isolated himself in meditation, sucking his comforter and with the corner of the pillow on his nose. Although he was a mischievous and lively boy, he had moments like this.

"I picked up the photo and read on the behind what was written in Father Jonathan's handwriting:

'Marine, what a lot of unforgettable memories this photo brings back! Memories that will remain alive forever to you and Alexandre.'

"The pain caused by Father Jonathan's absence got mixed up with the nightmare caused by such a tiny boy, who asserted he was Alexandre, the priest...

"My school was really the stage for a great act of the mysterious drama of my life..."

6) He cried on hearing "Última Canção" sung by Paulo Sérgio.

This popular song must have become engraved in Father Jonathan's memory. It was the one most often heard by Dona Marine and him when they were at the height of their relationship:

"August 25th, 1968: We went to the Priests' College. I saw Alexandre until the bus left. He said good bye and smiled."

"It was a painful day. After a few minutes of conversation with Father Jonathan in his sitting-room, while "**Última Canção**" was being played, he left to spend several days in B. H., studying and praying..."

D. Marine described how she felt on that cold and rainy afternoon, after the bus left taking Father Jonathan away.

On saying goodbye to D. Marine in his sitting room, and hearing the song "Última Canção", he must have felt the same emotion. Such moments are deeply felt by those in love, and become engraved in the memories of the ones who undergo this experience. The music associates itself to the moments lived under such emotions.

Let us return to the episode that happened with Kilden later, when he was still a child. In D. Marine's words:

"On another occasion, Marcinho bought us a record by the singer Paulo Sérgio. On listening to the first song "Última Canção" I noticed that Kilden, who was sitting on the sofa with the head in his arms, was crying.

'What's the matter? Why are you crying?' I asked him.

'The music makes me sad,' he said.

'Why, if you don't even know the music?

'Yes, I do. I'm Alexandre!' he cried."

As we can see, a song can evoke emotions and events from a previous life. It depends on the intensity of the emotion associated with it, as in this case.

These six items of the table of Kilden Alexandre's memories were taken from D. Marine Waterloo's Report and supplied by her.

* * *

After our visit to Kilden's delightful family we were pleased to get to know D. Marine personally, as well as her husband and children. We talked a lot with Kilden. He is a bright and intelligent boy. His reincarnation memories had practically disappeared. They began to fade when he was six years old, as is normal in cases of this nature.

However, some habits may persist, like tastes, traces of behaviour and characteristics that were typical of a former personality. Certain flashes of memory can also appear spontaneously. This happens when some fact or situation makes this possible, bringing the memory of outstanding events to consciousness.

During our visit we gave D. Marine a questionnaire to be answered in writing. We also had a long personal interview with her, as she was the person best informed about Kilden Alexandre.

After this visit, we started to exchange letters. We agreed that D. Marine would advise us, in writing, of all relevant facts observed by her with respect to her son's behaviour, as well as those episodes she remembered and that had not been recalled in her Report.

We have been successful in our written relationship with D. Marine. She has replied punctually, efficiently and willingly.

We will now transcribe relevant details regarding the Kilden Alexandre case, including the spontaneous memories he has had up to now.

OTHER RELEVANT DETAILS, RELATED TO BEHAVIOUR AND MEMORIES OF THE SUBJECT

(1) One of Father Jonathan's favourite pastimes was football. Kilden shows the same preference.

Father Jonathan was very fond of soccer. According to D. Marine, he set up twenty-two boys' teams and often played with them.

Kilden has the same fondness, in fact he is fanatical about soccer and his best means of enjoyment is playing soccer with the kids. As Kilden's father Marcinho says: "He is great with the ball".

(2) Another of Father Jonathan's characteristics was that he got on with people easily. Kilden has the same gift.

D. Marine emphasizes this resemblance of character between Father Jonathan and her son:

"Father Jonathan made friends easily with blacks, whites, poor, rich, men, women and children. My son is the same. He gets involved easily with people, and every time we go out we meet someone he greets."

(3) When Kilden was still very young, he used to say: "When I was grown-up..."

D. Marine mentioned this in her letter of December 27, 1990:

"After reading your book, **Reincarnation in Brazil**, I remembered that Kilden Alexandre used to say when he was still young: 'When I was grown-up...' I tried to explain to him that he had been even younger before, and that he had not been grown-up. I thought he was mixing things up, that he had no idea of what was young or grown-up."

It seems that reincarnation memories in children start approximately when they learn how to talk. Such memories reach their maximum intensity when they are around four years old. Then they decrease until they are six or seven, when they disappear entirely. However, there are exceptional people who retain traces of lasting memory, while others show signs of the behaviour and tastes that the personality had in the previous life.

Possibly, when still a child learning how to speak, Kilden tried to explain to his mother that he had been an adult. Later, when his vocabulary was richer, he started to complain when they called him by his first name – **Kilden**, saying he was Alexandre (see items 1 and 2 in **Table of Memories**). Finally, having learned more words, he was able to reveal his true identity (item 3).

4) Father Jonathan used to joke with rhyming words. Kilden has the same habit.

As pointed out by D. Marine in her letter of December 27th, 1990, this was one of his most remarkable habits, which could also be observed in Father Jonathan's informal chats:

"Nowadays my son remembers nothing, but his behaviour is similar to Father Jonathan's, who liked to rhyme words. He would say, for instance: "D. **Cléia** who likes **Geléia** (jelly)";

"**Marcia** who drinks milk from the **Bacia** (basin)..." and many other similar phrases. Kilden does not repeat what the priest said, but now and then he rhymes easily the words that somebody has just said. He often does this when we are coming back from school.

5) Father Jonathan made friends easily, but at the same time he made enemies due to his habit of playing practical jokes, some of them in poor taste. He was extremely extrovert and Kilden behaves the same way, causing quarrels with friends and with his own sisters...

"Kilden makes friends easily. He is very sociable, but some of his colleagues dislike him. His jokes with his sisters and starts fights. He makes jokes, his sisters cannot stand them and they end up quarrelling. Father Jonathan was disliked because of his jokes with the girls at my school.

"Kilden's father Marcinho works as a representative of a commercial company and has to travel a lot. Once, when he was in the city where Father Jonathan was born, he met Mr. Z. C., an old friend of this priest's family. He had known Father Jonathan since his childhood. Talking about when Jonathan was still young, he said it had been he (Mr. Z. C.) who had taken the boy, when he was a bit older, to the Seminary in N. P. where the future priest started studying. Mr. Z. C. said that Jonathan was a very intelligent boy, "but lived a life of fun. Only fun. The clearest memories of the youngster were his jokes." (Letter of July 5th, 1991)

Commenting on this fact in the same letter D. Marine says:

"I don't know if it is important, but I'm getting tired of my son's pranks. He not only has difficulty in learning but also takes everything as a joke. Let me explain: He has no problems in respect to discipline, neither in school, nor here in the Parish, where he is a member of the Dom Bosco Boys. Everyone likes him. They say he is not a problematic boy, he behaves well and is really polite. He is always ready to help and is very kind.

"His jokes start well, but irritate his sisters who end up quarrelling. After a quarrel, he begins to play with another one and so on. I remember that in the boarding school in N. P., Father Jonathan sometimes played jokes in poor taste, irritating some of the girls."

6) Kilden is extremely attached to St. John Bosco. Father Jonathan also worshipped this saint.

In the same letter of July 5th, 1991, D. Marine commented:

"Kilden likes Dom Bosco very much. He likes to receive postcards with his picture on them. A few days ago he was very happy when coming from a meeting with a large picture of St. John Bosco, which he had received and kept with great care, because he wanted to frame it. My eldest son had more contact with the Salesian priests, because he studied with the nuns, and went to the Parish during a long time before we moved to this district, but did not become attached to anything there, as Kilden did.

"Father Jonathan, who was a Salesian priest, often referred to St. John Bosco in his Sermons. The Salesian Congregation was founded by St. John Bosco in Turin, Italy, on January 26th 1854, when St. Francis of Sales was invoked; that is the reason why the religious congregation was named the Salesian Congregation.

This affection for Dom Bosco on Kilden's part, which was not induced by other people and seems inexplicable, suggests that he still has the same devotion that his previous personality showed – an unconscious impulse. It could be a "reincarnatory inheritance" of gifts, qualities, tendencies, etc. of a psychological nature, acquired by the former personality and passed on to the next personality. Buddhists call this sankharâ. The best definition of this word is: "...the dispositions or tendencies of this corporeal or mental mechanism, which allow the production of a result." (Oldenberg, 1921, pp.242-243; Andrade, 1984, pp. 203-204). The "sankharâs" also contribute in the building of people's "karma".

In Kilden's case, one immediately sees the influence of a "sankharâ" connected to his religious nature. In a letter, D. Marine Waterloo describes the following episode:

"Kilden Alexandre is always saying he is going to join the Air Force. As in January we moved to a district belonging to the parish of St. John Bosco (Salesian Priests), Kilden soon asked my eldest son to enrol him in the church, so that he could be an altar boy. The Salesian altar boys are known as "Dom Bosco's Boys" They play soccer and learn how to help celebrating Mass. Today was the first time Kilden participated in Dom Bosco's Church as an altar boy. I went to Mass to see him. On the way home he said: "You know, sometimes I think I won't join the Air Force after all".

I understand that we cannot analyse something that has not yet happened, yet I feel as a mother and a person who knows about these things that my responsibility is great. I said 'I know you are going to join the Air Force. But if you were a priest, what would you like to do?'

'Help people as much as I can' – he replied." (Letter of April 22nd, 1991)

7) At times, although Kilden has already forgotten his past life, he shows the conviction that he has been reborn.

Kilden goes to catechism classes as is usual for young Catholics, especially altar boys.

In the same letter of April 22nd, 1991, D. Marine writes:

"A few days ago, during catechism, he argued with the teacher, affirming that people are reborn – just as he was."

8) When he was ten years old and was asked about two people known to Father Jonathan, Kilden answered correctly about them.

In her letter of September 3rd, 1991, D. Marine describes the following episode:

"In 1990, I suddenly asked him if the name Deolinda meant anything to him. I was surprised by his answer: 'She was at N. P., I think she was a servant there'. We had never told him anything about Father Jonathan's family.

"On another occasion, a short time ago, I asked him: 'Kilden, who was Father A. L.?' He answered: 'He was a very old priest.' Quite right, Father A. L. was the Director of the Seminary when Father Jonathan was there. And in 1968, he was indeed a very old priest.

These are examples, of which there are more to come, of "sudden" remembrances that happen even after the disappearance of most children's past-life memories.

9) Kilden showed spontaneously a wish to study in the priests' boarding school.

From D. Marine's letter of November 18th, 1991:

"Kilden Alexandre wants to go to boarding school next year. He was so insistent that we tried to find out if still there was one in Cachoeira do Campo run by the Salesian priests. Last night I learned that there was one but we still don't know if he will be accepted, as he is going to repeat the third year in school next year.

"Everyone we know is surprised by Kilden's wish to go to boarding school, including our local vicar, who is his friend. Boys and girls nowadays don't usually like the idea of a boarding school far from home."

Further on D. Marine added: "Kilden insists that he wants to live in a boarding school with priests, but no one influenced him to take such a decision."

10) Without reason he showed a natural aversion to the name of one of his colleagues and a good friend of his.

D. Marine described Kilden's interest and paradoxical attitude in her letter of February 6th, 1992:

"A short time ago Kilden and I were walking down the street and in front of us was a colleague of his, together with her mother. He said: 'Mother, she's a nice girl! She is my friend. She's very nice but I don't like her name!'

I asked him what it was.

'Iara' he said. 'I think Iara is an awful name. What an

ugly name!' And he went on repeating the name saying that he didn't like it, and that it was an ugly name. I gave it no importance. I even said to him that it is a nice native Brazilian name. Two days later I suddenly remembered the name of the naughty girl at school who used to laugh at Father Jonathan.

Her name was Iara. Father Jonathan once asked me: 'Why does Iara hate me?' I didn't know the reason and he said: 'She has nothing inside that pate...' (He often used the word pate instead of 'head', a word that Kilden also used, although we don't have the habit of using it)"

This episode shows a fact that is often noticed in cases of reincarnation: phobia manifestations. The phobia may occur related to objects, colours, food, scenes, animals, words, etc. including names, as in this case.

11) He recognized a fruit called eugenia, a fruit that was abundant in the places where Father Jonathan lived, but was not to be found in the towns where Kilden and his brothers and sisters were born and grew up. So neither he nor his brothers or sisters had never eaten or seen such a fruit.

This episode was described in the same letter of February 6th, 1992, as follows:

"Another interesting fact happened on January 30th, 1992. I'll describe it according to my notes:

"Thursday, January 30th, 1992, Marcinho arrived from R.S. at 11 pm. We were awake and the children gathered around him.

"Marcinho then gave me a small package saying:

'What is this?'

"I opened it and almost screamed:

'Oh Lord, it's an eugenia!'

"Two enormous eugenias had been given to Marcinho in R.S. and he had brought them so that the kids might get to know them. They only grow where the climate is warmer. I knew them and sometimes I miss the enormous eugenia tree in the yard of my boarding school.

"Early next day Kilden Alexandre said:

'I remember eating that fruit a long time ago.'

'No, you never did. There aren't any around here.'

"He then said: 'Yes, I did. I'm sure father bought some us many years ago.'

'No, your father hasn't been travelling for a long time; he never brought us any eugenias.'

'Well, I don't know... but I did eat some many years ago.'

D. Marine then added the following note:

"No one around here knows this fruit, nor does Marcinho. Kilden doesn't know anything about the places my husband used to visit, or about Father Jonathan's home town. I chose not to talk about them, in order not to interfere with some spontaneous revelation."

It is interesting to see that although Kilden had apparently forgotten his reincarnatory experiences, he still kept them registered in a latent state.

This is a typical case of the phenomenon known as "déjà vu".

12) In April 1992, when Kilden was doing his homework in the classroom, an ambulance passed by with the siren going full blast. On hearing that sound Kilden showed signs of panic.

From D. Marine's letter of May 7th, 1992:

"About a month and a half ago Kilden was in the classroom, doing his homework when an ambulance went by at high speed with its loud siren going full blast. Kilden put his hand on his breast, turned pale and said: 'How sad. It makes me shudder.'

"Someone asked: 'What's the matter, Kilden? It's only the hospital ambulance.' They were going out to play but he didn't want to go, because he had a headache. He said he was scared. That evening, I thought about what had happened and decided to write a letter to Father Jonathan's sister-in-law, asking how the priest had been helped when he suffered the accident."

Several researchers are currently studying Near-Death Experiences (NDE). These studies became possible thanks to the great number of people that were "clinically dead" for some time, but were brought back to life thanks to recent resuscitation techniques. George W. Gallup and William Proctor carried out a survey in the USA in 1981, and verified that in that country about eight million people had already experienced a NDE. The pioneer in this field was Dr. Raymond A. Moody Jr., whose book Life after Life became an international bestseller.

Among the many surprising discoveries made by NDE researchers is that some of these patients in a near-death state remain entirely lucid and feel "out-of-the-body". In such a situation, they begin seeing the scenes and objects that are near them. They are able to hear noises and the talk of people nearby, or even at considerable distances. They usually see their own body stretched on the bed or on the operating table. There are many accounts of accident victims who have had the out-of-body sensation, and some have even followed the ambulance on its way to the hospital.

It is probable that, before finally dying, Father Jonathan may have gone through some of the NDE phases, seeing the removal of his body by the ambulance when he was being taken to the First-Aid Centre. He arrived there in a comatose state but only died the next day. It is probable that the scene of his rescue and the sound of the ambulance's siren impressed him strongly. If he had been out of his body, as frequently happens in NDE cases, he would have seen those scenes and engraved them strongly in his memory. The episode of the accident became associated with the blare of the siren and resurfaced in the emotion and feeling of panic in the classroom, as already described.

We have a confirmation of our hypothesis in D. Marine's letter of July 8th, 1993. (see item 19).

13) Kilden hates sideburns, as did Father Jonathan. Kilden's behaviour is identical to Father Jonathan's.

From D. Marine's letter of July 15th, 1992:

"I have noticed that Kilden has forgotten the things he

used to say when he was a small child, has no memories as he used to have of when he was a priest, but at times he behaves so like Father Jonathan that I feel like crying. For example:

a) "Combing his hair, many times I brushed his sideburns. He always got angry, saying he doesn't like sideburns and changed his way of combing his hair. I tried to tell him he looks nice, etc. He doesn't agree..."

"... Once, at school, Father Jonathan gave me a nice photo of himself. He was wearing a grey suit, and was smiling pleasantly. A few hours later, I waited for him near the chapel, in order to give him back the picture.

'Did you like it?', he asked.

'It is nice. It's a pity you don't have sideburns, though.' I replied.

'I don't like sideburns, can't get used to them.' he said.

b) "One day, when we were returning from school, Kilden said he wanted to live in B.H. (the city where Father Jonathan died), but because of the traffic it's a dangerous place."

c) "He is more full of fun than ever. An irritating joker, as Father Jonathan was, although he is more responsible and mature.

d) Continues to rhyme words, more and more.

From these reports we can see that there is evidence that our behaviour and, therefore, our "karma" seem to suffer the influence of our past lives. It is possible that each personality is made up of a mixture of genetic inheritance plus the "sankharâs", that is, the tendencies, qualities and deficiencies acquired in past lives.

Surely our qualities and deficiencies will suffer the influence of the place and the people with whom we live. From this exchange of actions and reactions our "karma" is born. The final result will be the change we will suffer in the future, by way of experience and progress, or stagnation and even moral relapse for a lifetime. In subsequent incarnations we will continue the process of improvement that each life offers to us, until we conquer the need to be reborn and return to the "samsarâ", that is, to the "vicious circle of successive incarnations".

14) According to D. Marine, Kilden is becoming more and more like Father Jonathan as he grows up.

From her letter of October 17th, 1992:

"I think it is interesting to note that as Kilden grows up, he becomes more and more like Father Jonathan. At times he argues and discusses as if he was a grown-up, although he does not remember perfectly what he studied in school."

She added that Kilden was taking the religious question very seriously, especially with regard to people's behaviour which, in his opinion, should be more in agreement with religious teachings. The Sister who taught the catechism told her that 'Your boy is charming. He is very responsible and always answers the questions I ask. He comments on the subject and is always attentive.'

At the same time, he continues to rhyme words as Father Jonathan used to do:

"More than ever, now he rhymes words all the time. He does it naturally. He doesn't know Father Jonathan had this habit" D. Marine writes.

15) In an informal chat, on giving his opinion regarding the worst way of dying, Kilden said it was that of being run over when you are cycling or on a motorcycle.

This episode was described in the same letter of October 17th, 1992:

"... Yesterday we were talking about Dr. Ulysses Guimarães' death and other kinds of death, when Késsia said she only fears being buried alive, dying of suffocation under the earth. Kilden got up and said:

"The worst death is dying in an accident! (He made a gesture with his hands as if he were riding a bicycle or a motorcycle, then opened his eyes wide). And he went on, speaking quite calmly: 'You're going along... then you get hit... and, boom... you're on the ground!' Késsia whispered in my ear: "I know you are thinking the same as I am". We didn't make any comments. This happened yesterday, October 13th, about 6:30 pm."

This episode shows the way the unconscious can influence our actions. The information stored in the mental archives of the spirit, referring to experiences suffered in past lives, at certain times can emerge in the conscious. For this to to happen, it is enough that an idea or an event strongly associated to it be invoked or provoked. A conversation or an identical situation may awake such a phenomenon of memory by association.

What happened to Kilden on that occasion serves as evidence supporting the reincarnation hypothesis. Since in this life he hadn't had any kind of accident with a bicycle or a motorcycle, his attitude seems explicable by this hypothesis. The accident that occurred with the previous personality

(Father Jonathan) became strongly engraved in the spiritual unconscious of the actual personality (Kilden). During our conversation, the memory of strong emotion that preceded the accident rose up to the conscious in the form of the expression manifested by the boy.

16) On happening to see a photo of the area where the two schools were situated, Kilden pointed out correctly the short cut that Father Jonathan used to take when he wanted to go from one to the other.

"Kilden pointed to the flowerbeds in the middle of the garden and said 'I'd rather go this way.' And Father Jonathan really used to pass that way."

"No comment."

17) Kilden spontaneously showed his desire to become a boarder at the Salesian school.

In the same letter of January 5th, 1993, D. Marine writes:

"His greatest dream is to finish the fourth year in order to study in C.P. as a boarder at the Salesian school. No one influenced him. He has been speaking of boarding school for a long time, and as there is only this one around here, he wants to win in order to get there next year. But I'm sorry for him, because he is not good at Portuguese Language and easily forgets what he learns."

It is interesting to note that although the former personality imposes its tastes and habits on the present one, it clashes with the physical and intellectual (or rather, cerebral) limitations of the latter's physiological equipment.

D. Marine constantly refers to the difficulties Kilden has in learning subjects taught at school. This shows that in addition to a certain level of evolution of the Spirit that is reincarnated, a corresponding organic quality is required in order for it to be able to show its abilities. There must be many geniuses around who are "prisoners" of bodies unsuitable for their manifestation.

On the other hand, there seem to have been many perfect organisms with excellent brains, but used by spirits of a low evolutionary level. These nearly always become the evil geniuses of mankind causing the great tragedies of history.

In Kilden's case, it is possible that the accident which caused Father Jonathan's death due to a blow on the head, may have influenced the structure of his brain. The intermission period (time between one incarnation and the next one) may have been insufficient for a total repair of the Biological Organizing Model. But these are only our suppositions. Besides, the repair work carried out by the "Perispirit", through the "Mental Body", goes on even after the spirit's incarnation. Thus it is possible to overcome congenital deficiencies, thanks to the spirit's resources. (Xavier & Vieira, 1959, Ch. II)

18) He correctly described the activity of someone he never knew but the priest did.

From D. Marine's letter of April 19th, 1993:

"I was telling the girls about the work of a youth group I had belonged to in the 1960s, and happened to mention one of its members called Orneles, whereupon Kilden said: 'He was a singer'. I was astonished because Orneles really was a singer. He composed the Group's songs, and rehearsed the chapel choir as well.

"In 1969 Father Jonathan went to B.H. and worked together with many groups in the slums, and I think that he got to know Orneles.

"It is interesting that when Kilden says something significant, it comes out spontaneously and confidently, as it has done before."

Kilden's case is full of fragments of memory that emerged by association of ideas. Facts like this help to explain the mechanism of the spirit's evolution, through the acquisition of qualities, and by the education and culture acquired during incarnations.

19) When he heard about somebody who had died after a fall from a ladder, Kilden explained how death occurs in cases like this. He also described correctly some phases of the Near-Death Experience, without having read or seen anything about it.

This interesting information is in D. Marine's letter of July 8th, 1993.

Here it is in full:

"Yesterday we lost one of our friends at the Institute of History and Geography. He was 74 years old. In the evening, Marcinho and I were talking about the last moments of a person, especially when they die as our friend from the Institute did: he was up a long ladder when it fell over, and he fractured his skull in four places, went into coma immediately and died five days later.

"Kilden then explained: 'It is like this: The person who suffered the accident arrives and is put in a room full of instruments. The doctors connect them...' (At this moment one of Marcinho's colleagues arrived and we left the two of them alone in the room). In the bedroom I allowed Kilden to continue.

"He went on: 'Then the equipment is connected to the chest and the head, and the doctors keep trying to save the life of the person. At this moment the person flies to a corner of the ceiling, watching the doctors' fight to save him. Then a big hole like a funnel appeared in the corner of the wall near me, trying to suck me...'

"Suck you, or the person who suffered the accident? I asked him.

"Very surprised, he said:

'Well, I think it was me. I saw my body and the doctors trying to save me.'

'It could have been in a film you saw,' I said 'or even a dream that you had.' But he said he had never seen a film like that, and that I could ask little Késsia. (They always watch films together because they get scared easily).

"Anyway, what happened to the person who suffered the accident?" I asked.

"When he was sucked through the hole into the tunnel, he saw a strong light at the end, so strong that I [sic] turned my head to one side. The light was very bright, and the hole closed behind him, near the wall. At that moment the doctors saw the screen on their machine stop. Then all the machines stopped working."

"When did you dream all this?

"I didn't dream it. I'm afraid of hurting my head... but we can see the doctors... Ah! When the hole was sucking the person in, the two most important doctors went over to the patient."

D. Marine Waterloo, discussing this episode of fragmented memories caused by association of Kilden's ideas, noted that it is the second time he has mentioned a First Aid room. These are her words:

"Dr. Hernani, this is the second time he has mentioned such a place since he grew up. But this time he gave a detailed description, and he was so impressed with the death of the man who fell off the ladder, that he is no longer goes up to the terrace to fly his kite."

Together with this letter, D. Marine sent us a drawing made by Kilden illustrating a scene where a person who suffered a fractured skull is being treated in a First Aid unit. Unfortunately the drawing cannot be reproduced.

A large rectangle represents the room. Inside it, on the left side, there is a smaller rectangle (the bed) with the figure of a person lying on his back. Behind the top of the bed is the equipment, one of the instruments being connected by wires to the bed where the patient is lying. At the side of the bed there are two small dark spots representing the doctors. On the right upper side of the larger rectangle there is a figure in a spiral, simulating the shape of a funnel starting from the interior corner and continuing on the outside. It is the hole or tunnel to which Kilden referred and that "sucked" him in. At the end of the tunnel there is something that represents the "very bright light" he saw.

From Kilden's normal behaviour one sees that he could not have obtained such meticulous details regarding a NDE. He does not read books about such matters, as he has difficulty in learning grammar. He also prefers playing soccer in the street with boys of his own age, flying kites, etc. He is not studious and doesn't like books. About the possibilities of his getting information from TV or films, D. Marine affirms that those were not the source of information. What remains is the emergence of memories of the event registered in his unconscious reincarnatory memory. It seems to us the best explanation.

20) Kilden remembered details of the Nuns' School where D. Marine met Father Jonathan. She had forgotten some of these details. (Letter of October 20th, 1993)

In this letter, D. Marine describes the episode in which Kilden, on seeing some photos, spoke of some details which she no longer remembered referring to the school she attended, where she came to know Father Jonathan. Here is the relevant part of the letter:

"I try to pass on to you only those remarks made by Kilden which I'm quite sure he had never heard or discussed here at home with me. Well, in that photo where you can see the Nuns' School, you can also see a eugenia tree in one of the school yards.

"We knew the place where it grew as the S.J. yard. The years erased from my memory one detail of this yard, which I continued to remember as the S.J. yard; it was not a playground, but was full of flowerbeds with the big eugenia tree in the middle. It had a door to my classroom, a door to the nuns' dining room, and another one to ours (which was not used); it had staircases to ... (can't remember) and to the nuns' dormitory. It had passages that led to the large yard, to the place where clothes were washed and part of the garden. I remember all this.

"But what is more surprising is that Kilden remembers precisely what I had forgotten. About two months ago he looked at the photos and said: 'Near that fruit tree there was a cave. It wasn't quite a cave but it was like a cave and it was near the tree. Remember, mother? It was grey and had a fence around it.' I then recalled the existence of something near the eugenia tree but couldn't remember exactly what it was.

"One afternoon I went to see Sister Luiza (an old Salesian nun). She had lived in the Nuns' School when I studied there. I asked her if there was a cave in the yard. She said no, but there was an image of St. John on a high pedestal, surrounded by a fence, and with a small entrance. She said the fence was of wood. Then I remembered that this small fence looked like roots and she agreed, though we doubted if the fence was really made of wood. I asked her about the colour of the image and the fence. She said that they were white but had got mouldy, darkening with time.

With an effort of memory, I recalled the grey details of the fence (it was made of plaited roots ending with a point, where the entrance was. Parts of the fence were rounded and rustic, like thick branches on which you could see some pointed marks. The fence was higher at the back, and lower on both sides of the entrance."

Dona Marine ends by saying that if she had done more to encourage her son to retrieve more memories from his past life when he first began to have them, she might have obtained yet more evidence.

EXTRACTS FROM THE QUESTIONNAIRE

When we visited Kilden's family on July 24th, 1994, in São João del Rey (Minas Gerais State), in addition to questions put to relatives and friends, we gave D. Marine Waterloo an extensive questionnaire. As it is very long and contains many redundant questions related to revelations already mentioned in the Report and in Dona Marine's letters, we will transcribe only what seemed to us more interesting or new.

We will list the most interesting questions and respective replies, adding our comments if necessary.

Initially we will try to obtain the most faithful description possible of the episodes in which the young Kilden revealed, decisively, that he had been Father Jonathan.

Question 1 – "Left Kilden on the bed, nearly naked, and went to the other room to take note of what he had said." Does D. Marine have the notes she took on that occasion? If so, could she give us the original or a photocopy of them?

A: As soon as I made a fair copy of the notes that I had taken in a hurry, I tore them up. I copied them as they were written down, and just as Kilden had spoken them:

"You know! I was on a motorcycle. Then a truck come and hit the motorcycle. I fell down, hit my head and died. I went deep down and then you got another me."

He said all this with his eyes wide open and a lively look on his face. And clutching my chin with his little hands, he repeated:

" After I went down deep in the hole, you got another me!"

I asked him when that had happened and he answered:

"When I was a priest! My motorcycle fell down to the ground, and I went down deep in the hole... and you got another me!"

Question 2 – Regarding the same episode, do you remember the date when you were giving Kilden his bath?

A: It was in 1983. I don't know the exact date. I wanted to commemorate something, because I had sent Kildary to my nephew's husband's bar, to buy a bottle of champagne. (It might have been August, or November 11th)

Question 3 - Is Mr. Jota Bueno still alive?

A: No, he died in 1985, after we moved to J.S.

Question 4 - Is Mr. J. S. Pereira still alive?

A: Mr. J. S. Pereira also died. He died before Mr. Bueno.

Author's Note: These two gentlemen were the directors of a Spiritist Group in the town in which D.Marine and her family were then living.

D. Marine did ask them for their comments on Kilden's revelations. (see the Report)

Question 5 - During the time you were pregnant with Kilden, did you have the wish to eat certain foods?

A: Yes. Most of the time I only ate potato salad, lettuce, tomato and cucumber. Everything with bread but without eggs or meat. I also ate a vegetable (similar to cabbage) called mustard, which I no longer like.

I always liked fried potatoes. I never liked them in salads but during this pregnancy I did, and as when it was over I didn't like them again.

Author's Note: Prof. Ian Stevenson reported that in some reincarnation cases, pregnant women's preferences coincided with those of the previous personality. (Stevenson, 1987, p.195).

In her letter of July 5th, 1991, D. Marine said that as her husband was a traveller, he used to go to Father Jonathan's birthplace. Once, when he was there, he went to see the priest's family and was very well received by his sister and niece. This is the part of the letter in which D. Marine refers to this episode:

"My husband said he has a friend who is writing something about Father Jonathan and that he would like to have some information regarding the priest's childhood and later life. They were delighted with the idea but had little to say. They said he liked vegetables, especially tomatoes (Kilden Alexandre eats raw tomatoes. Sometimes, even before I make the salad, he washes and eats them. But he won't eat them if they have received any seasoning.

In this case, Prof. Ian Stevenson's remarks were confirmed regarding pregnant women's preferences for certain foods. Although there is insufficient proof to establish an inductive and general law, in Kilden's case there seems to be a significant relation in the preferences with respect to food shown by D. Marine during her pregnancy with those of Father Jonathan when he was still alive. This fact adds one more piece of evidence in favour of the hypothesis that Kilden is the reincarnation of Father Jonathan.

Question 6 - Did you miss Father Jonathan more during your pregnancy?

A: No. I didn't. I was very grateful because I had asked his soul to help me pass the exam at the Institute for the Welfare of Minas Gerais State Workers. I got the first place and provided a mass for his soul. Soon after that I found out that I was pregnant.

Question 7 - Was Father Jonathan predominant in your dreams?

A: No I didn't dream of him.

Question 8 - What was your pregnancy like when you were expecting Kilden?

A: It was the most peaceful one, because I didn't have any kind of health problem. Kilden was born even before the doctor arrived.

Question 9 - Were the pregnancies of the other children very different?

A: Yes. I had a bad time in all the others.

Question 10 - Did any of the other children behave in a different way or say they were some other personality, or Father Jonathan?

A: No, none of them.

Question 11 - Do you still have dreams in which you see Father Jonathan?

A: I only dreamt of him once. I will copy what I wrote on August 27th, 1991:

About two months ago, when Marcinho and I were telling Kilden off because of his bad behaviour and his stubbornness, I dreamt that Father Jonathan came out of my wardrobe dressed in a black cassock and said "I'm suffering so much." I woke up frightened, and Marcinho at my side also woke up and said: "Marine, I think we should be more patient with Kilden. We should talk to the girls so that they can help. He is very much on his own" This is strange! Why, at the moment I had just finished dreaming, did he also wake up and say something so significant about Kilden? Marcinho does not believe in reincarnation or stories about Father Jonathan.

Question 12 - How are your dreams about Kilden?

A: They are sad dreams. I have dreamt that I was crying because Kilden had died, and that Marcinho and I had done nothing to save him. Once I dreamt that he fell in the river and that Marcinho, on the top of a hill, watched and smiled. I arrived, desperate, quarrelling with him. Then I woke up.

Most of my dreams about Kilden end abruptly. For example: he is falling into a hole and I wake up frightened; he dies and I become desperate, screaming, blaming myself and then I wake up.

The worst dream was the following one: I went into a small cemetery and saw an old man digging the earth with a spade. Then turning to Marcinho, who turned up near me, I said: "Poor little Kilden, he lived for such a short time and had no comfort in this life..." (It was Kilden's grave that the man was digging). Marcinho replied: "It's better this way". (This was the worst dream of all. I'm very afraid it might happen).

Question 13 - Does Kilden tell you his dreams? What does he dream about most often?

A: He often dreams about motorcycles. He always tells them to me, but nobody else.

A short time ago, the day before the exams, I woke him up early so that he could study. On getting up, he looked frightened and said: "Just as well you woke me up right before the accident!"

"What accident?" I asked him. Then, stretching out on his bed, he said: "Oh, Heavens! I was dreaming that I was among a lot of nuns, repairing my motorbike. I finished doing it and left, practically flying. When I was just going to hit the truck, you woke me up!"

During the day, he kept telling the dream several times.

Author's Note: Kilden's dreams have all reincarnation-memory characteristics. In our experience with reincarnation cases, we have come across this type of memory in dreams that are repetitive. They are known as recurrent dreams.

However, it is better not to let oneself be deceived by certain dreams that could be wrongly interpreted. In such false cases, usually the dreamers believe they could have been a famous personality in history.

The recurrent dreams that we verified so carefully, and considered to be evidence for reincarnation memories, are just like those Kilden had. They could be memories of former scenes connected to dramatic happenings that sometimes caused the death of the previous personality. (Playfair, 1976, pp 55-56;171-172).

Question 14 - How do you feel about your situation now that you have so much evidence that your son is the reincarnation of Father Jonathan?

A: I face it with much responsibility and also with much embarrassment. I know that Father Jonathan deserved to be born in a better home than mine, with a certain comfort and a more active social life, so that he (Kilden) could develop and continue the activities he had in his previous life, even if he was not going to be a priest, with a job of great value to the poor, as the priest had.

Question 15 - Do you still miss Father Jonathan?

A: Yes, mostly when I see in Kilden a similar behaviour to his. I don't miss him as much as I used to, it is different, a pleasant memory full of understanding and enjoyment of life.

Question 16 - Do you feel happy knowing that now he is your son?

A: Sometimes I do, because that feeling that brought us together overcame the frontiers of death and matter, and lives again in a gentle and loving boy, who is my son.

At other times I don't feel so happy, for several reasons:

1) Now and then Kilden causes bad feelings between my husband and myself. (They are things I can overcome, mainly because I understand a bit about the laws of reincarnation.)

2) Although he tries hard to get on with Kilden, Marcinho is still strict with him and mistreats him. To stop his father from slapping him, I myself have to punish him. This leads to confusion, because not understanding what is happening,

Kilden says: "Now it's mother who is angry with me, even before father begins. (These are difficult moments, which give no satisfaction at all).

Question 17 - Would you rather he had not reincarnated as your son?

A: I'm happy as things are. I know I have a very important mission, and am afraid I may have not the necessary strength to correspond to the numerous favours the Divine Plan puts in my way.

Question 18 - Would you rather ignore the fact that Kilden is the reincarnation of Father Jonathan?

A: I tried to do this for some years. I preferred to think that my mind had influenced the little boy, making him say those things.

Today I know that if I had kept the matter to myself, or pretended that it didn't happen, I would not have overcome all that I have.

Presenting Kilden's story during a class given by Mr. Luiz Brasil, just to get to know his opinion, was useful to all of us, especially for Kilden and myself.

I say so because now that I have a better understanding of where Kilden came from, who he was, and what might yet be, I can take decisions that will guide him in this world. If I had known nothing about reincarnation, Kilden might have been suffering due to his difficulty in remembering what he is taught. Now I know that it is not because of laziness. A broken head in a previous incarnation might cause a deficiency in a later one.

* * *

D. Marine Waterloo's answers to our questionnaire end here. Her answers were spontaneous and clear, and included some that touched on very intimate matters.

This singular "love story" now and then becomes dramatic, giving the impression that it is a work of fiction. However, the documentation that we have, which is available for examination, and that can be read at any time, is more than sufficient to convince those who are free from religious or doctrinaire prejudice that this exceptional case may be only a part of an extensive drama. The whole story may have been coming in for many years on the immense wave of a turbulent past, gradually reaching stages of less violence and suffering, like the foaming lacy waves that wash peacefully onto a sandy beach...

* * *

Let us leave such ideas for a moment and return to the subject of this monograph. Let us analyse the present case using hypotheses other than that of reincarnation. We must compare the reincarnation hypothesis with those generally used to explain cases similar to this one. This will enable us to evaluate the reincarnation hypothesis as an explanation of the case of **Kilden & Jonathan**, which is the aim of this book.

CHAPTER III

EXPLANATORY HYPOTHESES FOR KILDEN ALEXANDRE S MEMORIES AND BEHAVIOUR

"We think we depend on the body in order to live, but what happens is exactly the opposite: The body depends on us - what we really are - in order to exist. And when we leave this body behind, it immediately becomes waste, and a problem of which we must rid ourselves."

Levine, 1992.

The idea of reincarnation is a very old one. It forms part of the dogmas and teachings of nearly all great religions with the exception of Catholicism and Protestantism, yet in spite of the wide dissemination, in time and space, of the reincarnation doctrine there is still a persistent and systematic refusal to accept it. However, this difficulty in admitting the reality of reincarnation has diminished somewhat due to the appearance of psychotherapies based on regression to past lives. But in spite of the success of those who practice this kind of therapy, there are still those who do not admit that the positive results obtained in these regressive techniques are real evidence in favour of reincarnation.

This same reluctance is also observed in the cases of children who say they remember past lives. In order to justify this persistent scepticism, several explanations are offered to explain their mnemonic manifestations. We will examine the most common ones, and see if they can apply to the present case.

DELIBERATE FRAUD

This is the first hypothesis that sceptics propose, especially when cases of this nature are strongly supported by abundant evidence. The idea of the annihilation of the personality after bodily death is so ingrained in the minds of some, that even if they are presented with convincing facts favourable to survival after death, they cannot overcome their own incredulity. Reincarnation involves belief in survival after death. Therefore, the first barrier to its acceptance is the need to admit that life continues after death.

The idea of reincarnation is denied and even opposed by certain religions, especially Western Jewish-Christian ones. So even those who accept life after death, if they subscribe to one of these religions, will probably not accept reincarnation as an explanation for cases such as the one we have presented. So, faced with the facts, at first they deny the authenticity of them, and raise the possibility of fraud.

Let us see what would justify a fraud, and also the insistent manifestation and affirmation of falsehood in cases similar to the one we are presenting. Let us suppose that D. Marine Waterloo personally, or under pressure from her family, was hoping to become famous. This hypothesis cannot be sustained because D. Marine Waterloo asked us personally to take all necessary steps to protect her, her family and Father Jonathan's family, from the possibility of identification with those involved in this case. Thus, the names of places and people involved in this book have had their names deliberately changed by her. Hence the pseudonym of her choice, 'Marine Waterloo'.

Moreover, D. Marine's family showed little interest in, and even a certain opposition to publicising this story. Most of her family, especially her husband, are practicing Catholics. The eldest son is a seminarist about to be ordained as a Catholic priest. All these circumstances eliminate the hypothesis of family pressure, and also explain D. Marine's cautious approach.

Let us then think about the possibility of a hidden financial interest. This is the least sustainable hypothesis, in view of the difficulties in making a lot of money out of writing in our country. With very few exceptions the chances of making large sums of money as a writer here in Brazil are remote. Moreeover, when she authorised us (in writing) to include her Report in this work, D. Marine declared that she wanted no author's rights. She did so spontaneously, asking nothing in return except to remain anonymous.

It should also be borne in mind that D. Marine never tried to get in touch with us or with any other paranormal research association. It was Mr. Luiz Antônio Brasil who had this idea. D. Marine was surprised to know that other cases similar to hers have been scientifically studied without any religious implications. It was only when she got to know Mr. Brasil that she became familiar with this area of parapsychological research. Therefore, she would not have had the time or the technical ability to elaborate such a coherent plot just to become famous, or maybe to promote interest in "Scientific Spiritism" by making up a convoluted tale about reincarnation.

With respect to cultural and religious formation, D. Marine's upbringing was exclusively Catholic. Her husband and children are practicing Catholics, including Kilden Alexandre. It seems obvious that it would not be logical for her to make up such a story in order to get people to believe in something incompatible with their religion. Why would she do that?

Should there be another sufficiently strong reason to support the hypothesis of fraud, we confess we do not know what it could be, and would like very much to know what it is. However, due to our personal relations with D. Marine Waterloo and her family, we can testify that they are honest, modest and generous people who would be incapable of any deception.

DIRECT INFORMATION AND CRYPTOMNESIA

Cryptomnesia (from the Greek **kryptos**, hidden and **mneme**, memory) means literally **hidden memory**. In parapsychology it means the possibility of engraving on our unconscious all information obtained by our senses, including information not consciously perceived. We also include things which have been seen or experienced and apparently forgotten by our conscious or subconscious minds. In certain circumstances, the memory of information subliminally recorded or completely forgotten can rise to consciousness. In this particular situation, a person can become aware of facts and ideas, which apparently were never experienced or learned.

This hypothesis of **Direct Information and Cryptomnesia** could explain cases of apparent reincarnation memory.

In Kilden Alexandre's case, when he was very young he might have heard people talking about Father Jonathan in some detail. Even when the child was very young, he might have unconsciously registered such information in the form of hidden memory. When he started talking and was able to express himself in words, the child repeated what he had heard and registered in his unconscious, much to his mother's surprise.

This kind of explanation is easily accepted, as it seems logical, simple and scientific. It has come to seem obvious, even irrefutable. Yet it would be difficult to support it in the light of the facts presented and analysed here. If cryptomnesia worked with such ease, there would be no more illiterates and fools on earth.

Another strong objection to be considered is the meaning of words. A word is not merely an articulated sound. If it is to have any information content, it must be associated with a perceived fact, establishing a reflex of the secondary signalling system, or equivalent to another word with the same meaning for the one who is hearing it. Very young children can register sounds and their articulations as words or phrases. But these will only mean something to them when they are able to associate the sounds to facts perceived by their senses.

It would be difficult for a very young child to **understand** the meaning of the word **priest**, for example, without having seen one and learnt to relate the word to the individual dressed in a cassock. Even more difficult would be for a child to associate the word priest to a personal situation: "I am the priest!" (See item 2 in the **Table of Patient's First Memories**)

Let us assume that in spite of all these difficulties, Kilden was able to perform such a feat when he was two years old. It would be necessary to show that the detailed references to Father Jonathan were really so frequent. The priest had been dead for eight years when Kilden was born. If his mother mentioned the priest, she would have referred to him as Father Jonathan, not Alexandre which was their private pseudonym. So how did that two-year-old child know that Father Jonathan was also known by the intimate nickname Alexandre? Let us remember his remarks (item 2):

"I am not Kilden, you silly! I am the priest! I am Alexandre!"

D. Marine was so unaware of the extraordinary significance of these words that she did not appreciate at the time what they meant. They meant nothing to her. It does not seem, therefore, that she often talked about episodes that happened when she was at school or her conversations with Father Jonathan. And if she had, to whom would she have entrusted her intimacies, to the point of revealing the nickname Alexandre, which she and Father Jonathan had chosen?

Another puzzle would be why Kilden, when he was two years old, insisted so firmly that he was Alexandre, that he was the priest. Maybe direct information and cryptomnesia will not be able to explain this so easily? Even if we assume that such a fact, however exceptional, is explainable naturally in spite of the above objections, we will still face greater difficulties, as we shall see.

When D. Marine received the news of Father Jonathan's death, the information that she and her husband had was through the radio. Let us transcribe the part of D. Marine's report referring to this episode:

"I went in. But I had hardly closed the door when Marcinho, who was listening to Radio Guarani, went out to the street and called me. I went back to the shop.

"What was the name of that friend of yours, the priest?", he asked me as he turned off the radio.

"Father Jonathan", I said.

"He has just died in a hospital. He was in a **car accident** on Amazonina Avenue. He relapsed yesterday and died today."

This was what D. Marine wrote in her private diary on that occasion. The cause of Father Jonathan's death was a **car accident**.

Another relevant circumstance: The city where she and her husband lived was approximately 200 km from B.H.. The accident could not have been known about so soon and in detail, because the priest was not well known in her home town. So no one could give D. Marine any details of the accident. All she knew was that there had been a **car accident**, and she only got to know the details many years later, when she wrote to the institute where Father Jonathan spent his last years. By then, many years had gone by, and Kilden was four years old or more. It was not until later that D. Marine received Father Jonathan's biographical data containing details of the accident:

"On May 30th, on his way to the City Hall to request improvements for certain districts, he was run over by a truck in the Amazonina Avenue. His motorcycle got out of control and hit a Volkswagen that was waiting for the traffic light to turn green. So he fell over, hit his head on the pavement and fractured his skull..."

When Kilden was three years old, he described to D. Marine the details of the accident that caused his death in the previous life, which she did not know at that time. All she only knew was that Father Jonathan had been the victim of a **car accident**. This was one of the reasons that made her consult the institute in B.H. She wanted to make sure that the explanation she was given by the directors of the Spiritist Centre was correct, when she told them what her son Kilden had said. (See item 3 in the **Table of Patient's First Memories**)

In July 1994, when a well known psychiatrist friend of ours took a trip to the state of Minas Gerais, we asked him to interview Kilden's family. His interview of July 23rd with D. Marine, her husband and children, was recorded and filmed. Among the questions he asked D. Marine was one concerning her knowledge of the details of the accident that caused Father Jonathan's death. She confirmed that when Kilden revealed the details of the accident, she didn't know them. She only got to know them much later, after having written to the institution and received Father Jonathan's biographical data.

So we can see that there is strong evidence that, if any comments were made with respect to Father Jonathan during Kilden's first three years of life, none could have furnished sufficient details to justify the hypothesis of **direct information and cryptomnesia**.

Let us turn to another hypothesis raised to explain cases suggestive of reincarnation:

TELEPATHY, ESP AND SUPER-ESP

Extra-sensory perception (ESP) has been used to explain a great number of paranormal facts. It has been used especially in cases of mediumistic *transcommunications* (MTC), reducing them to telepathic messages obtained *mediumistically* from the minds of the family and friends of the person who died, who is supposedly communicating through the medium. It was this hypothesis that led Dr. Joseph Banks Rhine (1895-1980) and his colleagues to follow another path in their parapsychological research, suspending temporarily their study of mediumistic material. (Goldstein, 1985)

For reincarnation cases such as this one the ESP hypothesis has often been invoked. Those who accept this kind of reductionist explanation think that the **reincarnation** hypothesis is dispensable, as it involves survival after death, as well as the existence of the spirit, yet according to the reductionists, none of these postulates has been scientifically demonstrated. Therefore, such premises make the proposed solution hard to accept, as scientific method adopts the principles of William of Ockham (1300-1349) who, among other things, recommended that the most acceptable hypothesis should be that which requires the lowest number of postulates or assumptions. The law of parsimony, or 'Occam's Razor' states that "**Entia non sunt multiplicanda praeter necessitatem**" (Entities should not be multiplied needlessly.)

Now ESP has already been experimentally demonstrated in the laboratory, so it is a scientific fact and not an assumption. The existence of the spirit and survival, according to orthodox parapsychologists has not yet been scientifically demonstrated so they consider ESP a simpler explanation for mediumistic manifestation cases and also for those of supposed reincarnation memories.

For some parapsychology enthusiasts, the explanations by means of ESP go still further, as they accept the possibility of a "super-ESP" according to which there are no limits of time or space for direct cognition of the human mind, simply by "super-ESP".

We do not wish to tire the reader by seeking any further to reduce the value of this hypothesis. We refer those who are interested in this subject to pages 57-63 of our book: **Reencarnação no Brasil** (1988)

For those who do not wish to dig deep into the subject, we transcribe the following part of the above-mentioned work:

"Without a doubt, the possibilities of super-ESP are fascinating. It could be the key to explain everything and all forms of psi-gamma phenomena.

"With respect to this, Dr. Karlis Osis of the American Society for Psychical Research, makes the following comments:

'**One of the most fascinating characteristics of ESP is that it can overcome long distances in space, and seemingly in time also, penetrating the future.**'

"He adds that '**this apparent sovereignty of ESP over space and time has, over the centuries, spurred the creative imagination of researches and philosophers**'. Thus they claim that ESP '**gives back to man some of the dignity and grandeur lost in modern scientific concepts of personality.**'

"However, like others who have had direct contact with ESP research, Karlis Osis shows his scepticism about this question:

"The space-time problem has proved to be one of the

most dangerous pitfalls in parapsychology, because it has tempted researchers to speculate far beyond what our factual knowledge of ESP warrants." (Osis, 1965).

According to Osis, our knowledge about facts with respect to ESP and its relation to space and time is still uncertain. Osis has the authority to give an opinion about this question, since he has done a good deal of research into the influence of distance on ESP reception. He concludes, citing the work of numerous researchers, that distance does influence ESP, so it is inconsistent with facts to say that there is no space and time barrier that may influence ESP.

The eventual manifestation of super-ESP by exceptional sensitives would be only be evidence for their paranormal abilities. An analogy would be the resolution capability of a telescope or a microscope, which does not revoke the inverse of square of distance law that guides the distribution of the luminous intensity of a focus of light. (Andrade, 1988, pp. 60-61)

We do not want to deny "ab initio" the value of ESP in the explanation of paranormal facts similar to those we have shown, including the case that is being analysed. ESP could certainly be a more economical hypothesis for some of its features, for example items 4 and 5 of the **Table of Patient's First Memories**:

"Recognised spontaneously on a photograph some places where, as Father Jonathan, he had met D. Marine during their time at the Sisters' College."

In this episode, Kilden and his older brother Kildary picked up a postcard that had fallen down when D. Marine took some papers out of a box. Item 5 could also be explained by telepathy, as D. Marine was present when the boys picked up the photo. She observed for herself the behaviour of the boys when they looked at the photograph. But it is not quite clear why Kilden was the only one who showed so much interest in the picture, pointing with his finger to all places connected with the relationship between D. Marine and Father Jonathan. It also does not explain why only Kilden, and not Kildary, "captured" D. Marine's thought. She said that at that moment she missed Father Jonathan very much.

The details of Item 5, especially D. Marine's dialogue with Kilden, are even less clear if ESP is applied. When we consider the difficulties encountered in establishing evidence for ESP in a laboratory, we are not inclined to admit that a telepathic relationship can lead to a dialogue. Moreover, to prefer the ESP hypothesis to others, we would have to introduce many more postulates than the simple reincarnation hypothesis requires.

How can we explain items 1, 2, 3 and 6 of the **Table of Subject's First Memories** by telepathy? How can we avoid "Ockham's Razor" in these instances?

Let us examine the **Other Relevant Details in the Subject's Behaviour and Memories**. How can we use ESP in items 1 to 20, especially item 19?

Apart from ESP's inability to explain the above-mentioned items, it is totally unable to answer the questions in **Extracts from the Questionnaire**.

We think the examples presented should be sufficient to conclude that telepathy, ESP and Super-ESP cannot definitively explain the case of Kilden and Father Jonathan.

GENETIC MEMORY

Jean Baptiste Lamarck (1744-1829) was a brilliant man with wide-ranging interests. He originally intended to be a priest, but when he was 16 years old he chose a military career. After being wounded, he decided to leave the army, moved to Paris and entered the College of Medicine. Later, he was to become a world famous naturalist.

Lamarck became interested in animal evolution and created the theory that bears his name. Very briefly, his **Zoologist Philosophy** (1809) establishes that: 1) The continuous use of organs fortifies them and promotes their development; but when they are not used they atrophy. 2) **The characters acquired during the existence of living beings**, resulting from the exercise of their organic functions, **are transmitted to future successive generations**, through heredity.

The **hereditary transmission of acquired characteristics** became controversial and was denied by Science, after **Alfred Russel Wallace** (1823-1913) and **Charles Robert Darwin's** (1809-1882) discoveries and their joint communication at the Linnean Society in 1858 entitled **About the Tendencies of Species to Make Varieties and About the Varieties and Species Perpetuation Through Natural Selection Processes**.

On November 24th, 1859, Darwin published his book **About the Origin of the Species Through Natural Selection Processes or The Preservation of Favoured Races in the Fight for Life**. (Darwin, 1981-1982)

In accordance with investigations made by **Wallace** and **Darwin**, the characteristics acquired by individuals during their lives **are not transmitted** by heredity to their descendants.

The differences that occur in individuals of a certain lineage have their origin in the chance alterations that occur in the **chromosomal genes** of the germinative cells. When the variations result in qualities favorable to the mutant's survival, such new characteristics tend to maintain themselves in their descendants, until genetic alterations by chance happen again during later generations. The same process of selection of the fittest continues. In this way, the species will change, creating more favourable and functional new qualities, according to a continuous process of evolution, as well as a slow adaptation to the conditions of the environment in which they live.

For many years certain breeds of dog had their tails cut when they were very young. Now, their descendants are always born with a normal tail, without atrophy or any other signal. This is an example showing that the characteristics and physiological modifications acquired during the life of a certain species **are not** transmissible by inheritance to their descendants.

However, if certain individuals are exposed for a long time to high energy radiation, modifications in the chromosomal genes of their sexual cells might occur. In this case, it might cause the appearance of new favorable or disadvantageous characteristic in their descendants. But such mutations are unpredictable and will not correspond to any modification in shape and somatic quality of the progenitors.

When one mentions **genetic memory** as an explanation for cases that suggest reincarnation, such as the one we are analysing, we have to assume that there could have been a hereditary transfer of acquired psychical experience from the parents to their descendants.

In Kilden Alexandre's case, for example, could the memory of the dramatic moments lived by D. Marine have been genetically transferred to her son?

Although this hypothesis might seem absurd, as it represents an attempt to revive Lamarck's theory, it has been invoked in order to replace that of reincarnation. Supporters of the explanation based on genetic memory look to animal psychology for support. This theory is thoroughly examined in our book **Reencarnação no Brasil** (Andrade, 1988, pp.63-78). We suggest this source of information to those who wish to know more about the problem. However, we feel it is needless to repeat the arguments we used simply to refute the hypothesis of genetic memory to explain cases that deal with apparent reincarnation.

Even if genetic memory accountd for "acquired psychic characteriteristics", the hypothesis could not explain any of the items of the **Table of Subject's First Memories**, nor any of the **Other Relevant Details in Subject's Behaviour and Memories**, with the exception of items 8, 11, 16, 18 and 20. Therefore we consider it pointless to persist in using this kind of explanation for this case.

We will now pass on to the next hypothesis.

MEDIUMSTIC INCORPORATION

This explanation could be proposed by spiritualists or by parapsychologists who already accept the fact that spirits exist and can communicate, but who do not admit reincarnation, especially in a case such as that of Kilden Alexandre.

The hypothesis of **mediumistic incorporation** could explain several items of the table of the subject's behaviour and memories. However, the phenomenon of incorporation on the part of Kilden would have to have assumed unheard-of characteristics of permanent possession and absence of the necessary symptoms of trance.

We have long personal experience (about 50 years) of the phenomenon of mediumistic incorporation. When this happens it usually causes typical changes in the personality and attitude of the medium, which make it easily identifiable. The description given by D. Marine, regarding things that happened with Kilden when he was identifying himself as Father Jonathan, who had already died, shows no sign of mediumistic incorporation. Even when he said he was the priest and that his name was Alexandre, all we can see is a child's behaviour in the confused phase of reincarnatory memories. If this had only been an instance of mediumistic incorporation, he would have behaved as an adult and said: "I am Father Jonathan" and nothing else, keeping calm and showing no sign of irritation. (see items 1 and 2 of **Table of Subject's First Memories**)

The dialogue between Kilden and D. Marine when the episode of the bath happened (item 3 of the same table), is typical of a child in a normal state when talking to his mother. The words used by Kilden show clearly how a

3-year-old child would use them in order to explain a fact which had occurred under those conditions and with his limited available vocabulary. In no way is it typical for an adult incorporated in a medium. He would have identified himself as Father Jonathan and used other words. Over and above this, he would not have used the expression: "When I was a priest." but he would have said: "When I died and my name was Father Jonathan, etc, etc." If he wanted to identity himself and communicate with D. Marine, it would be more logical that he would have done so in this way, introducing himself with his real identity, and not as a child treating her as a mother.

The **mediumistic incorporation** hypothesis also does not explain the rest of the items of the **Table of Subject's First Memories**.

As to the **Other Relevant Details in Subject's Behaviour and Memories**, a permanent possession by the spirit of Father Jonathan of Kilden's body would be necessary. Such an idea cannot withstand the most elementary logic.

Also, during a visit we made to the family, we had the opportunity of talking to Kilden for a long time, during which we were able to observe him closely. He didn't show any signs of mediumistic ability, nor of being someone easily possessed. He is a bright, intelligent and absolutely normal boy.

We do not believe that the **mediumistic incorporation** hypothesis explains Kilden Alexandre's case.

REINCARNATION

Belief in reincarnation requires the acceptance of two premises: 1) The survival of the spirit after the death of the body and 2) The return of the spirit to corporeal life by means of a new birth.

Denial of the first condition eliminates the possibility of acceptance of the second one. However, it is possible to believe in survival after death, yet not to believe in the possibility of the spirit returning to life by means of a new birth here in this world.

In such circumstances it is not possible to demonstrate scientifically the reality of reincarnation solely on theoretical principles. The evidence supporting the idea of reincarnation must be based on facts. Empirical demonstration of the reality of reincarnation will support the belief in survival after death and in the rebirth of the spirit.

Belief in reincarnation is very old, and also seems to have started with the observation and registry of cases of proven memories of past lives, like the one we are studying in this book.

Nowadays it is not only the cases of people who spontaneously remember having lived one or more previous lives that have claimed the attention of investigators. Some researchers have been trying to awake such memories in ordinary subjects, using different methods such as hypnosis, association of ideas, trances, meditation, drugs, etc. Among these researchers into reincarnation, we distinguish two categories:

1) Those who use hypnosis followed by suggestions in an

attempt to make their subjects go back in time until they pass beyond the embryonic stage and reach one or more past lives. They are only interested in information concerning reincarnation. (Lorenz, 1948; Bernstein, 1956; Guirdham, 1970 and 1973).

2) Psychotherapists who use regression to past lives in an effort to cure certain psychosomatic illnesses or psychic anomalies. This therapy is now widespread. There have been hundreds of studies on this matter from all over the world. (Fiore, 1981; Netherton & Shiffrin, 1978; Pincherle and others, 1985; Wambach, 1981; Tendam, 1990; Wiesendanger, 1994)

Although this kind of investigation has furnished a good deal of evidence in favour of reincarnation, sceptics have also criticized it, as have other psychologists and psychiatrists. The more radical ones ascribe the claimed memories of past lives to fantasies or to facts seen, read or watched on films, TV soap operas, etc., which remained buried in the unconscious of the patients. They could be the result of normal creativity or cryptomnesia.

There are indeed some cases that have been found to have alternative reductionist explanations. There are others for which the best explanation currently available has been shown to be the reincarnation hypothesis.

Among the categories of investigation in cases that suggest rebirth, the one which in my opinion presents the best evidence in favour of reincarnation, is the one that examines cases of memories of past lives manifested in **very young children**.

One of the pioneers of this type of research was Prof.

Hemendra Nath Banerjee (1931-1985). When we got to know him personally in 1970, Prof. Banerjee had already collected about 600 cases of children who remembered past lives. (Banerjee, 1964, 1965, 1974, 1979, 1980, 1986)

Nowadays the most important researcher in this category of reincarnation cases is **Prof. Ian Stevenson**, from the University of Virginia in Charlottesville, U.S.A. He is a retired psychiatrist and holder of the Carlson Chair in Psychiatry of the Medical School of that University. He began his research in 1961, when he went to India to study **cases that suggest reincarnation** in that country. From that year up to now he has extended his investigations to cases of the same category in several countries other than India, including Brazil. At the moment his enormous collection has over 2500 such cases, and he has published many works describing and analysing them in detail. (Stevenson, 1966, 1974, 1975, 1977a, 1980, 1983, 1987). He is highly respected in the scientific world; proof of this respect is the acceptance his works have had among publications of recognized prestige, such as the **Journal of Nervous and Mental Disease.** (Stevenson, 1977b)

These few examples show that the reincarnation hypothesis is not a mere religious dogma, nor a simple idea born of unfounded suppositions arbitrarily invented to explain enigmatic facts. Even the Egyptians and other ancient peoples knew about reincarnation. Pythagoras (570-496 BC) brought the idea from Egypt to Greece. (Muller, 1970, pp. 20-23)

We shall now pass on to an evaluation of the results and the applicability of the reincarnation hypothesis as an explanation for the case that we are analysing.

If we admit that Kilden is really the reincarnation of

Father Jonathan, all the items of the **Table of the Subject's First Memories**, as well as all items of the **Other Relevant Details in the Subject's Behaviour and Memories** are fully justified. We should add that even such minimal details as the following ones would be clarified:

1) The intermission period of 7 years, 11 months and 24 days between Father Jonathan's death and Kilden's birth is well within the statistical average of the period during which children remember past lives, here in Brazil and in the rest of the world. (Goldstein, 1991)

2) Certain episodes which occurred even after the fading of Kilden's memories and related behaviour, are quite explainable; for example: a) his religious tendencies; b) Item 19 of the **Other Relevant Details in the Subject's Behaviour and Memories**, in which he describes an **NDE experience**.

3) Modifications to D. Marine's eating habits during her pregnancy, similar to those of Father Jonathan. (see Question 5 of the **Extracts from the Questionnaire**)

On re-reading the Analysis of Evidence and considering the validity of the reincarnationist hypothesis, the reader will clearly notice a compatibility of this position with the nature of the documented facts.

To conclude, the reincarnation hypothesis is the one that, up to now, best accounts for all aspects of this case. Until a more adequate explanation is provided, the reincarnation hypothesis is still the one that best applies to this case.

Therefore, the evidence that Kilden is the reincarnation of Father Jonathan remains robust.

CHAPTER IV

EPILOGUE

SUDDENLY YOU WENT AWAY

(To J.)

Suddenly,
You said Good-bye,
and the Gross Matter
transformed you...
Suddenly,
you went to sleep,
a chaos surrounded you
and it all ended...

Suddenly!
So suddenly,
that I couldn't believe it!
But Life
is made up of happenings
and our dreams
are suspended,
as we see our loved ones
Being destroyed one day...

No...
Your body did not say goodbye...
But your soul,

flew to me,
called me
and smiled!
And said that everything stopped...
and that a new life was born!...

Not understanding
the splendour of eternity,
I cried so much!
So many useless lives!
Just you,
death turned into dust!?

But, from the rosy Mansion,
to me,
you stretched your hand,
and, shining,
I could see you!
No more suffering...
No more poverty,
nor pain
for the pains of world!

You said you are well
and that one day,
to the Eternal Joy
I will also go!

(Marine Waterloo)

AN EXPLANATION

The reader may find the **epilogue** chosen to close the present case somewhat strange. As this is meant to be a strictly scientific book, it should either have ended after the previous chapter, or have had a formal, rational and objective conclusion. This book, like those already published by us about cases that suggest reincarnation, has obeyed the same ethical criteria of strict impartiality that were applied to those that preceded it.

However, the present case, besides having a purely scientific aspect, has a component of sentimental, dramatic and deeply human nature. Within it there are two people connected by strong mutual affection. Once reincarnation is demonstrated, at least in the case we are studying, it seems to show clearly that the feelings which intervene in human relationships are perpetual. As we can see, this is the main ingredient in the complex composition of what we know as "karma".

We have enough experience with the scientific "establishment" to calculate the risk we are running of invalidating the present work, or reducing its value and credibility, just by pointing out this aspect. We know very well that a work which wishes to be truly scientific should be **cold** and **impartial** in addition to being strictly faithful to the facts. However, we feel it appropriate to end this work on a human rather than a strictly scientific note.

BETWEEN THE LINES

From the many letters received from D. Marine, as well as from the answers to the questionnaire submitted to her, one fact stands out:

Although she is convinced that her son Kilden is the reincarnation of Father Jonathan, she maintains two kinds of affection for the two personalities. She loves Kilden as any good mother loves her son, yet she still has a deep affection for Father Jonathan, missing him sorely.

How can we explain this sentimental duality?

This fact teaches us that there is a real but **formal** difference between the **personalities** manifested by the same spirit in its successive incarnations. We said **formal**, in the sense of the **causes** that originate people. We are reminded of the four categories defined by Aristotle: material cause, **formal** cause, efficient cause and final cause. It is the **form** and not the substance that produces in us the immediate concept of the difference between the **personalities** assumed by the same spirit in its various incarnations. For this reason, we can love the same spirit in different ways, depending on the personalities manifested by it when it is incarnated. Perhaps this is the reason for the duality of feelings shown by D. Marine Waterloo for Father Jonathan and Kilden.

Our spirit is an **individuality** that passes from one incarnation to another, gradually enriching its stock of information and experience. Each life is a lesson that is learnt; it is also another step in the direction of its liberation from the need to return to the "samsarâ" (vicious circle of successive reincarnations). Consequently, the individuality also changes, generally perfecting itself; it develops. It can also stall and even regress morally, but this is uncommon.

When not guided by higher powers, spirits tend to return to the same group of individuals who are similar to them. In this case, the group goes on through time and space, weaving their stories together, their dramas, their "**karmas**". Their hatreds, revenges, interests, affinities, friendships and **loves** are the objectives of nearly all reincarnations. It is the **final cause** that attracts the spirits to a new birth experience.

We should here remember Buddha's words:

"Oh disciples, which do you think is greater, the waters of the immense ocean or the tears that you have shed as you erred in this long peregrination, precipitating yourself from new births to new deaths, bound to those you hate, separated from those you love?"

(Samyutta Nikaya)

It seems that the case we have been studying is only a tiny detail of a far bigger drama; the "tip of an iceberg..."

Let us repeat a passage of D. Marine Waterloo's **Report**:

"The night was high, and through the window the Moon could be seen in the limpid sky. The stars, so distant, bathed in moonlight, were not as beautiful as the leaves of the palm trees close to our dormitory. The lawn of the yard seemed to sparkle, and in the silence of the night, only cut by the murmurings of my colleagues, my fingers, arms and body bean to swell... My breathing stopped from one moment to the next because of a strange anguish that felt like death. I lay on my bed and tried to breathe deeply, turning towards the window, but a weakness in my knees and arms almost paralyzed me. I opened my mouth, trying to swallow the largest amount of possible oxygen, but it was all in vain. This feeling was not new to me, but every time it happened, it frightened me even more.

"While this bizarre phenomenon lasted, a different moonlight invaded my memory; a big house, like an opulent palace, and a luxurious room was drawn to me, however without showing me many details... In that room there was a repugnant scene that I didn't manage to understand (though I was forced to accept it) and a strange and very white man who did not look quite normal...

"Such scenes didn't appear clearly enough to make my search through my memories, trying to discover some similar incident in my childhood, or in any reading that I have done. Yet they did not come from books, nor from my childhood. I was the adult woman in that luxurious room, the main character in that absolutely clear scene.

"It was something real, lived by me, that my memory couldn't quite catch up with it."

In a further letter D. Marine described in more detail such experiences of apparent memories of scenes seen in supposed former lives. Here is part of hers of June 19th, 1994:

"I would really like to know about my past. I feel that I have had a few little hints that, if I had been able to follow them up, might have explained many things.

"I also believe that I am a very old spirit, who has lived thousands of times on this Planet and hasn't developed very much."

It is obvious that if reincarnation is a law of nature, as it really seems to be, then all living creatures, especially those of our species, must have been reborn many times. But there are people that, in a more pronounced degree, feel they have lived before. Some of them remember better than others. However, there are some that never have had such 'memories'.

Could past-life memories be no more than fantasies?

We believe that most of them are really mental creations, repressed desires that free themselves by means of this kind of daydream influenced by fashion - nowadays this topic is widely discussed.

But there are cases that suggest the reality of a new birth, as in the case of **Kilden & Jonathan**. Dr. Ian Stevenson and Prof. Hemendra Nath Banerjee came across thousands of cases of this nature.

And how can one explain the success of cures brought about by **regression to past lives?**

WOULD LOVE BE LIKE SPRING?

What is it that makes it easier to recall some past lives than others? Could it be a violent drama, suffering, tragedy - or a simple love story?

In the case of Kilden and Jonathan it seems that a pure and intense affection can cause the return of the spirit to a body, in search of the object of its love.

If this is a general rule, those who love each other deeply and are suddenly separated by the death of a partner should not despair. The parents who lost their children, the wife who lost her husband, the sweethearts separated by the death of a companion, in short all those who weep for the loss of those they loved who went to the other world should dry their tears.

They did not disappear forever, because there is much evidence that Love is like Spring - they both always return...

THE END

BIBLIOGRAPHY

ANDRADE, H.G. (1976) Jacira & Ronaldo. Um Caso que Sugere Reencarnação. São Paulo: IBPP. See also: Reencarnação no Brasil. Matão: Casa Editora O Clarim Cap. III, pp.82-124, 1988a.

ANDRADE, H.G. (1983) Morte, Renascimento, Evolução. São Paulo: Pensamento.

ANDRADE, H.G. (1986) Psi Quântico. São Paulo: Pensamento.

ANDRADE, H.G. (1988a) Reencarnação no Brasil. Matão: Casa Editora O Clarim.

ANDRADE, H.G. (1988b) Poltergeist. Algumas de Suas Ocorrências no Brasil. São Paulo: Pensamento.

BANERJEE, Hemendra Nath (1964) Munesh Report of the Case Suggestive of Extra-Cerebral Memory. Jaipur, India: University of Rajasthan.

BANERJEE, Hemendra Nath (1965) Review of a Case-History Suggestive of Extra-Cerebral Memory. (Prabhu Report of the Case Suggestive of Extra-Cerebral Memory); Jaipur, India: Rajasthan University Press.

BANERJEE, Hemendra Nath & OURSLER, W. (1974) Lives Unlimited. New York: Doubleday.

BANERJEE, Hemendra Nath (1979) The Once and Future Life. New York: Dell.

BANERJEE, Hemendra Nath (1980) Americans Who Have Been Reincarnated. New York: Macmillan Publishing.

BANERJEE, Hemendra Nath (1986) Vida Pretérita e Futura. Trans. Sylvio Monteiro; Rio de Janeiro: Nórdica.

BERNSTEIN, Morey (1956) The Search for Bridey Murphy. London: Hutchinson 1956, New York: Doubleday, Garden City. Revised ed. (1965) São Paulo: Pensamento.

DARWIN, Charles (1981) A Origem das Espécies, trans. Eduardo Fonseca; São Paulo: Hemus.

DARWIN, Charles (1982) A Origem das Espécies, (illustrated), condensed and trans. by Richard E. Leakey: São Paulo: Univ. of Brasilia/Melhoramentos.

FIORE, Edith (1981) Já Vivemos Antes, trans. Maria Luisa Ferreira da Costa; Lisbon: Publicações Europa-América.

FODOR, Nandor (1974) Encyclopaedia of Psychic Science. U.S.A.: University Books.

GOLDSTEIN, Karl W. (1985) A Moderna Parapsicologia. Folha Espírita, July, São Paulo.

GOLDSTEIN, Karl W. (1991) "Quanto Tempo Dura a Morte?". Folha Espírita, December, São Paulo.

GUIRDHAM, Arthur (1970) Os Cátaros e a Reencarnação. São Paulo: Pensamento.

GUIRDHAM, Arthur (1973) Entre Dois Mundos. São Paulo: Pensamento.

LEVINE, Stephen (1992) "O Que Sobrevive?", in Gary Doore, Explorações Contemporâneas da Vida Depois da Morte. São Paulo: Cultrix.

LORENZ, Francisco Valdomiro (1948) A Voz do Antigo Egito. Rio de Janeiro: FEB.

MERCIER, Évelyne-Sarah (1992) La Mort Transfigurée. Paris: L'Âge du Verseau.

MOODY Jr., Raymond A. (1975) Vida Depois da Vida. Rio de Janeiro: Nórdica.

MOODY Jr., Raymond A. (1977) Reflexões Sobre Vida Depois da Vida. Rio de Janeiro: Nórdica.

MOODY Jr., Raymond A. (1988) A Luz do Além. Rio de Janeiro: Nórdica.

MOODY Jr., Raymond A. (1992) Investigando Vidas Passadas. São Paulo: Cultrix.

MORSE, Dr. Melvin & PERRY, Paul (1990) Do Outro Lado da Vida. Rio de Janeiro: Objetiva.

MULLER, Dr. Karl E. (1970) Reincarnation Based on Facts. London: Psychic Press.

MULLER, Dr. Karl E. (1978) Reencarnação Baseada em Fatos, trans. Harry Meredig. São Paulo: EDICEL, (see pp. 21-25).

NETHERTON, Morris & SHIFFRIN, Nancy (1978) Past Lives Therapy. New York: William Morrow.

OLDENBERG, H. (1921) Le Bouddha, Sa Vie, Sa Doctrine, Sa Communauté. Paris: Félix Alcan.

OSIS, Karlis (1965) "ESP Over Distance". Journal of the American Society for Psychical Research, January 1965.

PINCHERLE, L.T., LYRA, A., SILVA, D.B.T., GONÇALVES, A.M. (1985) Psicoterapias e Estados de Transe. São Paulo: Sumus Editorial.

PLAYFAIR, Guy Lyon (1976) The Indefinite Boundary. London: Souvenir Press.

RAWLINGS, Maurice (1979) Beyond Death's Door. New York: Bantam Books.

RING, Kenneth (1992) The Omega Project. New York: William Morrow and Company, Inc.

RITCHIE, George G. (1980) Voltar do Amanhã. Rio de Janeiro: Nórdica.

RUYER, Raymond (1974) La Gnose de Princeton. Paris: Fayard.

RUYER, Raymond (1989) A Gnose de Princeton. trans. Liliane Barthod. São Paulo: Cultrix.

SABOM, Michael B. (1982) Recollections of Death. London: Corgi Books.

SIDGWICK, Eleanor Mildred; GURNEY, Edmund; MYERS, Frederick W.H.; PODMORE, Frank (1975) Perspectives in Psychical Research. New York: Arno Press and University Books. (This edition combines 'Phantasms of the Living' by Gurney, Myers and Podmore (1886) with Sidgwick's 'Phantasms of the Dead' originally published in the Proceedings of the Society for Psychical Research, Vol. III, 1885).

STEVENSON, Ian (1966) "Twenty Cases Suggestive of Reincarnation". Proceedings of the American Society for Psychical Research, Vol. XXVI, September 1966.

STEVENSON, Ian (1974) Twenty Cases Suggestive of Reincarnation. 2nd edition, revised and enlarged. Charlottesville: University Press of Virginia.

STEVENSON, Ian (1975) Cases of the Reincarnation Type. Vol. I, Ten Cases in India. Charlottesville: University Press of Virginia.

STEVENSON, Ian (1977a) Cases of the Reincarnation Type. Vol. II, Ten Cases in Sri Lanka. Charlottesville: University Press of Virginia.

STEVENSON, Ian (1977b) "The explanatory value of the idea of reincarnation. Journal of Nervous and Mental Disease, 164;305-26.

STEVENSON, Ian (1980) Cases of the Reincarnation Type. Vol. III, Twelve Cases in Lebanon and Turkey. Charlottesville: University Press of Virginia.

STEVENSON, Ian (1983) Cases of the Reincarnation Type Vol. IV, Twelve Cases in Thailand and Burma. Charlottesville: University Press of Virginia.

STEVENSON, Ian (1987) Children Who Remember Previous Lives. Charlottesville: University Press of Virginia.

TENDAM, Hans (1990) Exploring Reincarnation. London: Arkana.

TYRRELL, G.N.M. (1973) Apparitions. London: Society for Psychical Research.

WAMBACH, Helen (1981) Recordando Vidas Passadas. trans. Octavio Mendes Cajado; São Paulo: Pensamento.

WIESENDANGER, Harald (1994) A Terapia da Reencarnação. trans. Zilda Hutchinson Schild Silva; São Paulo: Pensamento.

WILBER, Ken (1992) "Morte, Renascimento e Meditação" in Explorações Contemporâneas da Vida Depois da Morte. São Paulo: Cultrix.

XAVIER, F. C. & VIEIRA, W. (1959) Evolução em Dois Mundos. Rio de Janeiro: FEB.